Praise for *Spiritual Activator*

"Oliver is a gifted healer whose energy-healing practices would benefit those looking to experience more joy, inner peace, and wellness in their lives."

— **Tony Robbins**, #1 *New York Times* best-selling author of *Life Force*

"From the moment I connected with Oliver, I felt his energy, passion, and caring for all of us who have the possibility to be released from the traumas and issues we emotionally hold on to. The wisdom and psychic energy that he teaches and shares are so special. Thank you so much, Oliver, for your compassion and passion for us all."

— **Donna Karan**, fashion designer

"Oliver is a gifted soul who has the ability to change someone's frequency by activating their true essence and voice, which can be buried under trauma, pain, and suffering."

— **Anthony William**, Medical Medium, #1 *New York Times* best-selling author of the *Medical Medium* book series

"Thank you, Oliver, for your continuous generosity in helping me raise my energy so I can experience a more expansive and beautiful life."

— **Julianne Hough**, American dancer, actress, and singer

"The main theme of my work as a storyteller explores the concept of ordinary people becoming extraordinary. What Oliver has achieved in Spiritual Activator is to create a tangible guide for this exploration by providing practical tools to discover and harness the extraordinary power that lies within all of us."

— **Tim Kring**, television producer and creator of *Strange World*, *Crossing Jordan*, *Heroes*, and *Touch*

T0286318

SPIRITUAL ACTIVATOR

SPIRITUAL ACTIVATOR

5 STEPS TO CLEARING,
UNBLOCKING, AND PROTECTING
YOUR ENERGY TO ATTRACT MORE
LOVE, JOY, AND PURPOSE

OLIVER NIÑO

HAY HOUSE LLC
Carlsbad, California • New York City
London • Sydney • New Delhi

Published in the United States by: Hay House LLC: www.hayhouse.com® •
Published in Australia by: Hay House Australia Publishing Pty Ltd: www.
hayhouse.com.au • *Published in the United Kingdom by:* Hay House UK
Ltd: www.hayhouse.co.uk • *Published in India by:* Hay House Publishers
(India) Pvt Ltd: www.hayhouse.co.in

Project editor: Melody Guy
Cover design: 99 Designs
Interior design: Alex Head / Draft Lab
Interior photos/illustrations: Liezl B., Authentic Living

Cataloging-in-Publication Data is on file at the Library of Congress

Tradepaper ISBN: 978-1-4019-7402-2
E-book ISBN: 978-1-4019-6772-7
Audiobook ISBN: 978-1-4019-6773-4

10 9 8 7 6 5 4 3 2 1
1st edition, March 2023
2nd edition, September 2024

Printed in the United States of America

This product uses responsibly sourced papers and/or recycled materials.
For more information, see www.hayhouse.com.

For Mandy, Bray, Zi, and new baby.
You are all my "WHY."

And for all those who have followed me
throughout the years, your stories and
transformations drive me to reach more souls
and shine more light into this world.

I love you all.

CONTENTS

Introduction xi

PART I: UNBLOCK TO DETOX

Chapter **1**: Gifts, Healing, and Serving Others. 3

Chapter **2**: Why Do I Need to Detox?. .27

PART II: YOUR 15-DAY PLAN

Chapter **3**: Days 1–3: Protect Your Energy 49

Chapter **4**: Days 4–6: Clear Your Energy. 71

Chapter **5**: Days 7–9: Elevate Your Energy 97

Chapter **6**: Days 10–12: Discover Your Gifts 119

Chapter **7**: Days 13–15: Practice Your Abilities and
Purpose Work 149

Afterword: Spread the Blessings 169

A Special Invitation:
Join the Spiritual Activator Soul Family 171

Acknowledgments 173

About the Author. 177

INTRODUCTION

HAVE YOU EXPERIENCED ANY of the following?

When you are out in public, you find yourself greatly affected by other people's energies, so much so that you might feel overwhelm, frustration, anxiety, or panic and you just want to deeply feel peace, calm, and clarity.

You (or a loved one) are experiencing chronic pain or debilitating disease, and you've tried everything you can to get better and get answers but nothing seems to work consistently and permanently.

Unexplained things have always happened to you growing up, and no one has been able to give you answers as to why. Maybe you dream about things and they end up coming true, or you just "know" stuff and you don't know how or why. Or maybe you see other dimensions or get "messages" from the other side.

You feel drained toward the end of the day, and people just seem to take, take, take from you all the time. You seem to attract toxic or negative people in your life who drain you of your energy and vitality, and you just want to feel GOOD again.

You are going through a spiritual awakening, and life feels like a roller coaster. You are searching for answers to a lot of questions, and for some reason you just can't get any clarity or resolution.

You know that you're "different" from everyone else. You are in tune with a whole other world of energy and spirituality; you know there's more to life than meets the eye, and you are ready to explore that.

You have experienced the "dark night of the soul," and you're ready to turn the page to the next chapter of your life because deep down you know you are here for something bigger even if you don't know what it is.

If you resonated with any of these scenarios, then this book was written specifically for you.

You see, I've experienced these situations myself. I've gone through them all, and I'm now at the end of the tunnel. Not only is there light at the end of the tunnel, but it's not really the end at all—it's a new beginning. You're not at the end; you are going through to the other side.

On the other side is a life full of purpose, joy, love, happiness, peace, bliss, clarity, and wholeness, and I'm here to show you how I got here, step by step, so you can break free from the invisible energy blocks that have been holding you back.

Spiritual Activator: 5 Steps to Clearing, Unblocking, and Protecting Your Energy to Attract More Love, Joy, and Purpose is a fun and simple solution to help you break through your life's confusing discord. My program takes the guesswork out of why you feel the way you do and removes crippling blocks from your energetic field that stand between you and abundance. You already know about the popular healing benefits of green smoothies, liver cleanses, and detox diets. Well, it's as important to cleanse your energetic body as it is your physical and mental ones. By doing this, you eliminate any issues at their energetic roots, which allows your body to become a clear vessel for divine frequencies to flow through it. This energy can give you the guidance you need to examine and claim your spiritual gifts, pursue your purpose, and thrive.

Energetic blocks slow down, dampen, or stop your ability to be the best version of yourself—and my detox removes the cumulative, negative energetic effects of bad experiences on your physical, emotional, spiritual, and energetic bodies. In this book, I'll explain how energetic blocks lodge themselves in your system as negative beliefs, emotions, and sometimes even physical conditions. Traumas, ancestral roots, or environmental factors create feelings of fear, guilt, anger, betrayal, uselessness, hurt, and inadequacy that can flow through you like dangerous free radicals. These create walls in your energetic field, which can cause physical disease, relationship issues, feeling stuck, a lack of abundance, a lack of purpose, a lack of confidence, anxiety, depression, and/or a general feeling of unhappiness. Certain factors keep that energy alive, including negative beliefs. When you cleanse, or remove, the blocks that weigh you down using my healing techniques, it not only detoxes your energetic fields—thus, healing various aspects of wellness—but it allows you to tap into a higher power and activate your gifts so you can pursue your purpose. You are wired to clear your energy field. Your soul arrived here in a clear, energetic state, so the universe encourages you to return to your natural way of being.

This detox program is divided into two parts. Part I will offer background on my story, energy healing, and why it's so important to energetically cleanse your system, while Part II will outline the specific steps you will take during your 15-day cleanse. The program consists of just five powerful steps, with three days devoted to mastering each. You will first learn how to protect, clear, and elevate your energy, and then discover ways to explore your gifts and pursue your purpose work. Each three-day block offers various exercises, tools, and meditations for you to use and eventually determine, via trial and error, which work best for flushing out your system.

As you progress, you'll layer the practices, adding to those from the days prior, so that you're collectively creating a set routine that positively changes your energy, and eventually, your entire life. If you fall off the cleansing wagon, simply pick up where you left off; and after finishing the program, if you ever feel energetically cloudy or your spiritual gifts seem rusty, just repeat the detox. I have clients who like to cleanse every 90 days or so to keep their energy in its most pure and fluid state. My program is designed to be versatile, personal, and intuitively based, so once your 15 days with me are over and you've learned what makes your system feel its best, you're now the expert on your body and capable of deciding how to support your energetic flow.

In just two weeks, your physical, emotional, and energetic bodies will undergo vast improvements as you cleanse your field from blocks and contaminants, plus learn how to sustain this clearer state. *Spiritual Activator* will invite peace, happiness, and abundance into your life.

I've been called a lot of things in my adult life: an energy healer, spiritual activator, lightworker, influencer . . . but the truth is, I'm a pretty normal guy whose out-of-this-world spiritual awakening led me to my soul's mission: rescuing humans like you from suffering, as fast as possible, and helping them experience their truest, and most empowering, potential. I've spent close to 20 years performing energy healings and reaching millions of souls and sharing with them how to detox their own energy so that they can create the life they desire—and one that's always in alignment with the universe's highest good. In my program, Geo Love Healing, I help individuals master their energy, unblock themselves from mental, emotional, and energetic blocks, and become certified healers and life coaches. I lead workshops, spearhead events, and teach online sessions to students from all over the world. They experience results quickly, and I strive to be authentic and supportive during their journeys. I've performed over 20,000 healings and trained close to 2 million students online, from over 60 countries. I receive thousands of e-mails each month from awakened souls who share their success stories with me. All of this is why I know my energy detox and other spiritual tools work. If you stick with my program, they'll work for you too.

When it comes to energy healing, I'm mostly self-taught, which is intentional. I want to be sure that the messages I channel and lessons I teach are as potent and pure for others as they were for me when I first received them. These techniques channel through me, but they are not originally mine. They come from a higher power. It is simply my responsibility to share what has changed my life, as well as the lives of countless clients. I am a messenger for divine wisdom that has existed for a very long time. I use this information for the highest good of all so that I can make a difference and give back to the world. I've been shown that energetic detoxes are an essential first step for anyone determined to operate from their highest self too.

No matter what their station in life, all my students, like you, long to understand their emotional pasts, spiritual gifts, and purpose work. They include billionaire business magnates, presidential families, medical professionals, body workers, ex-military with PTSD, psychologists, first responders aiming to supplement their practices, health and wellness practitioners, teachers, electricians, parents, and the diverse list goes on and on. When my clients first come to see me, most don't know what energy healing is and why it's so instrumental to feeling fulfilled, joyful, and at peace. I teach them that when you learn to detox your energy, it affects every detail of your life. A pure energetic field makes or breaks relationships, home, sleep, health, job, finances, you name it—and an energetic reset eliminates the environmental, ancestral, and emotional toxins that hold you back from being your healthiest self. Once you've cleansed all of this negativity, your recharged energy opens the door for exploring and practicing your spiritual gifts and discovering your purpose work. This feeds and gratifies your soul.

Bonus: You'll see sacred geometry images that were channeled by my sister Liezl sprinkled throughout the book. You can use these for protection, meditation, or to set an intention if you feel a connection with them.

Ready for this wild ride? I promise that when we're finished, life will never be the same, in all the best ways. I can't wait for you to experience the best of what life has to offer.

A Quick Word about God

In *Spiritual Activator*, I will talk about God a lot. Although I was raised Catholic, I have expanded my understanding of what God is and think of God as a gender-free source of energy rather than an all-powerful man with a thick, white beard who sits on a fluffy cloud in the sky. To me, God is the limitless energy source from which all life begins and ends. I also believe that in God's universe, our souls reincarnate into multiple lifetimes so that we can learn lessons each time—and sometimes on planets other than Earth. In fact, I believe that multiple timelines exist at once, since time is a man-made concept. Because of this, I also believe that you can teleport yourself to other versions of your life, if you know the right practices to do so. I mention these mind-bending concepts because I reference them in the book, and I want to make sure we're on the same page.

Though I use the word *God* to refer to our universe's energetic source, other common terms for God include Source, universe, the divine, higher power, and others—so I may use these terms interchangeably. I also like to use the term your highest self, which describes the part of your soul that is wisest, most aware, most potent, and most connected to God. Your highest self is what links the material world to the mystical. It helps determine your course as an embodied being on earth. Your highest self is also the version of you that has all the answers and is equipped with a lot of spiritual gifts.

PART I

UNBLOCK TO DETOX

Chapter 1

GIFTS, HEALING, AND SERVING OTHERS

WHEN I WAS YOUNGER, I rarely felt comfortable in my skin. I always felt stressed out, hopeless, stuck, sad, and different from everyone else. I turned to popular self-improvement tools, hoping they'd point the way to inner peace and prosperity, but my efforts came up flat. I recited affirmations, dissected and revised my limiting beliefs, read tons of self-help books, and went to therapy. Yet no matter how much I "did the work," my life either stalled or got worse.

It wasn't until I learned about the energy in and around our bodies, and how keeping this energy cleansed can unveil and sharpen our spiritual gifts and purpose in life, that everything changed.

Big time.

Turns out that taking care of your energetic body is as essential as caring for your physical, mental, and emotional selves. No matter what your background or religious beliefs, energy affects you—deeper than you can imagine. The key to happiness, peace, and fulfillment, then, is purifying and mastering your energetic body. As soon as I learned to do this, life began to work *for* me, rather than *against* me. I became more confident, vibrant, loved, and at one with God. I felt like the person that I always knew I was and tried so hard to share with others. I now attracted incredible friends, partners, business prospects, and a lifestyle that I felt I deserved—while toxic people and opportunities fell away. Acceptance, abundance, and success were no longer dreams but a daily reality. Achieving the impossible became not only inevitable but a daily lifestyle. Miracles and blessings now show up so often that strangers who watch it play out joke that a day in my life feels like a movie, but it's all become normal to me. It's been nearly 20 years since I first discovered the extraordinary power that comes with understanding, detoxing, and using energy to create a life I never dreamed was possible. This kind of joy, abundance, and clarity are *your* soul's natural way of operating too. Let me explain how I got there, so you can recognize where our stories converge—and with this book, experience the universe's magic for yourself.

A SPIRITUAL HEAD START

I'm originally from the city of Manila, which is the capital of the Philippines. If you've never been, I like to compare my hometown to New York City—an urban playground full of skyscrapers, tourists, and a diverse class system. I lived there until I graduated high school. At the time, most of the locals spoke English, including my family. I think the best reflection of the city's population might actually be its restaurants—Chinese, Italian, Japanese, French, Middle Eastern, you name it. Outside the city, the general landscape is more provincial and underdeveloped. It reminds me of the Texas or Arizona countryside, where you can drive for miles and see nothing but cows and farmland.

Catholicism was, and still is, the predominant belief system in the Philippines, so it's no surprise that I grew up in a fiercely Catholic family. The funny thing about Filipino culture, though, is that it's big on superstition too. So like many Filipinos, my family leaned in to spiritual practices that weren't religious whenever it suited us. Like when we'd move to a new home, my parents would hire an albularyo to bless the land; he might also be called on if a family member was sick with a tough illness or in an unshakably dark mood. The word *albularyo* translates to medicine man, folk healer, or witch doctor. As kids, my friends and I also wore agimats—amulets or charms made of brass, copper, wood, or bone—which are related to Filipino magic and sorcery. We believed the threaded talismans brought us good luck and kept us safe with their mystical powers. So on the one hand, out-of-the-box spiritual practices were considered taboo, but on the other, they were embedded in our culture. You can imagine how this sent me mixed messages as a child, even though mystical contradictions exist in most cultures. It's like how old-school Italians can strictly practice Catholicism, which condemns supernatural beliefs, but might wear a cornicello, which is Italian for horn, around their neck to protect them from the evil eye.

Not only did my family lean in to these cultural practices when the spirit moved them, but they possessed innate supernatural gifts that some of my friends' families didn't. When I was young, my paternal grandfather, who we called Lolo, often channeled the souls of dead relatives, but only when he felt it was necessary. When my family fought over a land inheritance, Lolo channeled his

5

deceased father to settle the rivalry. Lolo also called on deceased family members for heavenly advice and insight to solve health concerns. When he channeled, his head would fall back, his voice would get deeper and slower, and his mannerisms would look just like the souls that he'd conjured. If, as a human, the soul was tall, Lolo would pull his shoulders back to make himself appear larger than life, or if it had a limp or lisp while alive, he'd mimic that too. The soul would then say its name and deliver the message. It was scary and fascinating at the same time.

My parents also demonstrated gifts, so these sorts of abilities ran on both sides of my family. My father spoke in tongues, which he felt was an acceptable and blessed gift from the Holy Spirit, though I now view his gift as him channeling energy by using his tongue to communicate its sound frequency. Meanwhile, my mother dreamed warnings, mostly about family members' accidents, deaths or unfaithful spouses, and her dreams all come true. Once she dreamed that my cousin's fiancé got into a freak car accident; two weeks later, his car was tragically hit and he flew through his windshield and died.

And then, every once in a while, we'd experience spiritual phenomena and startling interactions with mythical beings. Once, during the anniversary of my maternal grandmother's death, all my family members smelled her strong perfume, no matter where we stood in the room; we could also smell her favorite flower, the distinctly sweet and fragrant sampaguita, the national flower of the Philippines. Similar to how the Irish have leprechauns and Icelanders have elves, in Filipino folklore there is the Kapre. The Kapre isn't cute and playful. It looks like a giant, gnarled tree and is typically tall, dark, hairy, and very muscular. Kapres are also believed to smoke cigars and have strong, terrible body odor. They like to play pranks on people or befriend women they find attractive. When my sister Pia was seven years old, she swore she heard a Kapre's deep laugh and voice beckon to her; she immediately ran away screaming. When she told the adults, everyone believed her and then shared their own stories about Kapre sightings.

This might sound like it made for fascinating barbecues or family reunions, but there was still a lot of fear and shame around believing in spiritual oddities that weren't condoned by Catholicism. Even so, they piqued my curiosity, especially when, around the age of seven, I began to have my own curious encounters. For one, I sensed things that my friends and classmates didn't. I instinctively knew what people around me thought and felt, picked up on the presence of spirits in the room, and saw silhouettes of angels and other light beings. I'd feel goosebumps, my heart would race, and then I'd suddenly feel a tug between fear and fascination. Fright typically won out whenever this occurred, so I learned to shut my spiritual abilities down by ignoring my sixth sense and staying busy with school. I also prayed a lot, when I wasn't smoking cigarettes and swigging from a bottle of lambanog, a Filipino hard liquor. Drinking numbed me out enough to take the edge off and weaken my spiritual antennae, which I now know is because it dims the chakras and third eye.

As time went on, I became increasingly reclusive and didn't fit in with most of the kids at school because I didn't feel "normal." I worried that others could sense that something was different about me. I became an outcast who was often bullied and forced to eat my lunch in the boys' bathroom. I'd find an empty stall, lock the door, sit on the toilet lid, and lift my feet up so nobody would know I was there. Had I known my gifts were a blessing, and that I could control them, perhaps I would have felt less terrorized and ashamed. Looking back, I would have given anything for a guide of some kind to provide context to what I was experiencing—someone who could tell me that these traits made me special, not strange. I'd like to think I would have used my gifts to understand the other kids around me on a deeper level and help them understand me too.

NEW COUNTRY, NEW ME

When I was 18 years old, my family moved to the United States. In the Philippines, my mother was an established pediatrician, while my father wore a lot of hats—surgeon, dentist, real estate mogul, and soldier in the Philippine Army. Before our move, though, my father focused mostly on being a businessman. He grew many different kinds of rice and sold them in large barrels at our local market and in over a dozen cities. Though his business did well for a while, it eventually fell on hard times and our family accumulated a lot of untenable debt. That's when my parents decided to move us from Manila to Lakewood, California, for a fresh start. Both of my parents became nurses and worked hard to offer me and my siblings a better education and more opportunities than they felt we'd have access to at home.

Just before we moved, I was learning how to fit in by becoming a musician. I played guitar in a band and wrote a lot of moody, romantic songs. It was a safe outlet for me, since musicians are usually popular, so it scored me friends and even my first girlfriend. But in Lakewood, I was a stranger in a strange land and had a hard time adjusting. I had no friends and couldn't relate to the culture. I decided that I had no choice but to use the move as an opportunity to reinvent my identity. I also badly needed money, so I launched an online business that specialized in relationship and dating advice for men. I was good at giving advice to the guys in the band, thanks to the fact that I have four sisters; and around the same time, the movie *Hitch* with Will Smith had come out, so offering romantic tips from a guy's perspective was in the zeitgeist. I taught seminars and workshops, published e-books, sold digital programs, and did all the company's marketing. Running this site helped me meet a few new friends and feel less lonely. At the same time, I dug into self-development books and growth work. I listened to CDs, went to workshops, and read self-help books like Napoleon Hill's *Think and Grow Rich*, Dale Carnegie's *How to Win Friends and Influence People*, and Earl Nightingale's *The Strangest Secret*. I tried hard not to feel as lost as I did as a kid in Manila.

About two years later, I talked to my co-worker Jeff about everything I'd learned in the self-help arena and how I'd been trying to apply it to the business—but I wasn't too sure if it was helping. He suggested I connect with a psychic named Christel, who could offer some spiritual guidance and supernatural insight about my goals. I was desperate to do anything I could to find happiness and success. A little mysticism couldn't hurt—and in fact, it spoke to the Filipino side of me that was raised in a culture that welcomed the occasional spiritual intervention.

During my reading, Christel zeroed in on energy blocks in my chakras and auric field, which is an energetic halo that extends 18 inches, or more, around everyone's bodies. She said these blocks were stopping me from reaching financial and emotional abundance—and then drew me a picture of where they lived, relative to my energetic body. Christel also talked to me about chakras, which she said are spinning disks of energy that refer to energy points in the body and correspond to bundles of nerves, major organs, and areas that affect our emotional and physical well-being. This was the first time anyone had talked to me about energy, much less how it related to social and financial fulfillment. It felt like I'd been handed a secret, magical key, and I planned to use it to open as many doors as I could.

When I left Christel, I felt newly hopeful and excited for the future—and if working on my energy was a super-highway to happiness, money, and fulfillment, I was eager to learn as much as I could. Christel then told me about a healer named Nick who could sense *and remove* my blocks, which would help me become the best and most productive version of myself. I couldn't book that appointment fast enough.

When I met Nick, I was fascinated by and drawn to his new age vibe. He lived in a guest house in Malibu on Topanga Canyon; the house itself was shaped like an octagon, which I've since learned is a spiritual symbol for rebirth and eternal life. In Nick's sacred space, posters of deities like Ganesh and Amma, who is referred to as "the hugging saint," hung on his walls. Meditative music and the smell of newly burned sage filled the room. Nick was very tall, dressed in all white with mala beads around his neck, in his mid-30s, and had an Australian accent, though he barely spoke. He simply pointed to a chair for me to sit in, then asked me to close my eyes as he waved a smoky quartz crystal around my body and made whoosh-ing sounds with his mouth. Though my eyes were shut, I peeked sometimes to see him use various crystals to remove the blocks that he said had been holding me back for so long. Our 40-minute session felt relaxing, but I didn't feel much other than calm and open to more spiritual experiences. At the end, Nick said a great opportunity would bring me abundance in three to five weeks. I crossed my fingers and looked out for sudden good fortune.

SPIRITUAL AWAKENINGS

About a month later, I got a call to participate in an opportunity that would make me more money in one day than I could in over a year—and I instantly attributed it to Nick's healing. (I couldn't explain it otherwise!) I was asked to speak at a conference packed with thousands of guests, eager to buy a program that I created to help them grow their company's social media followings. I hadn't done anything different in my life or career to welcome this invite, other than to see Nick, so I trusted that his clearing removed enough blocks from my field to allow abundance to flow from the universe. Unfortunately, because I'd never made this much money in my life, *much less in one shot*, I was irresponsible and lost most of the cash, and soon I was right back to where I began.

Despite that, I wanted to forge a new path for myself and couldn't look away from the miracle I'd experienced— and with such minimal effort. I intuitively knew I needed to know more about how Nick's abilities worked so I could use them on myself. We kept in touch and became friends as I picked his brain about chakras, healing, and energy. Between Christel and Nick, I learned a lot of the basics involved in healing work: details about grounding, protection, energetic cords (invisible cords that connect you to others through thoughts, emotions, feelings, and physical sensations), auras, chakras, and of course, energetic blocks. I still use and teach a lot of these tools today—and I'll get into them much deeper later in the book.

Once I exhausted my mentors' knowledge, I remained hungry to learn more and determined to understand as much as I could. It's like that old saying, "Give a man a fish, and he will eat for a day. Teach a man to fish, and he will eat for a lifetime." I craved a lifetime of good fortune and spiritual alignment that flowed freely from energy healings. I couldn't help but suspect that the universe had dangled a carrot in front of me by guiding me to these two spiritual teachers who seemed to hold the keys to success, as my gut said I could do this work on my own.

I was in search of life-changing tools that would help to improve my work and guide my spiritual journey, so Christel recommended I travel to Sedona, which she said was the hub of spiritual growth and enlightenment. She said it was a magical, mystical city—one where I could learn, ·grow, and unblock even more energetic impediments.

While in Sedona, I hired a shaman tour guide at Christel's suggestion, which became the highlight of my trip. This man really knew the spiritual lay of the land. He took our group to the top of vortex points, where tourists are said to have spiritual awakenings, and explained that a vortex point is any point on earth that acts as a swirling center of earthly energy, containing more energy than other points in the world. The Great Pyramid in Egypt, Machu Picchu in Peru, and Stonehenge in England are other vortex points said to hold the same mystical power as those Arizona mountaintops.

I climbed to the peak of a small vortex point, closed my eyes, and sat quietly. Almost immediately, I was overcome by a very strong energy that rose up from the earth and into my body. I was lightheaded and tingly throughout my whole being, and I felt myself emotionally crack open. My eyes flooded with tears, as deeply traumatic experiences bubbled up to the surface of my mind and consciousness— around abandonment, rejection, self-love, guilt, resentment, and anger. These were mostly from old wounds related to my family and upbringing. I harbored a lot of bitterness toward my parents for moving to the U.S. just as I was getting comfortable in Manila. I felt like the rug had been pulled out from under me. Because I felt so displaced in a new culture, I also dealt with feelings of inadequacy rooted in those childhood bullying days, plus not knowing how to succeed in circles so different from what I was used to.

While on our vortex points, our guide said that if we felt overcome with painful emotions, we shouldn't fear them but lovingly release them into the earth. The best way to do this was to notice these emotions without judgment and say, "I'm releasing and letting go for the highest good of all." So when my burdens surfaced, I let them go. I also intuitively suspected that these were the root causes of even more energetic blocks that hadn't yet left my auric field and needed to be set free. I mentally imagined handing them to the earth, and since I was doing this on a vortex point, I believed it would be a swift and intense process. After I released these feelings, I pictured a cup of dirty water emptying out within myself that allowed me to make space for a newer, purer energy to come into my being. Once the cup was empty, I felt a strong jolt of energy pass through me—and that's when the visions started.

Sacred geometry symbols appeared in my mind's eye out of nowhere. Unfamiliar shapes and patterns flooded my thinking—and, I'll be honest, I momentarily wondered if I was dehydrated from being out in the sun too long! Earlier that week, I had noticed a few locals wearing similar shapes on a necklace, scarf, or shirt, but I never realized that these were sacred geometry that held special meaning.

After a half hour, I opened my eyes. The symbols disappeared—but they were replaced by the physical presentation of energy playing out before me. The energy looked like sparkles, almost like fireflies, and I could move my hand over and through them, as if they were a hologram. I saw atoms split and spirals of light dance in the air. I believe I was witnessing an energetic realm that few can see. I instinctively knew that I had opened my third eye during this vortex point meditation, and that my life was about to change.

I believe those moments on the mountaintop initiated a clear connection to a higher power, because the images and visions kept coming. It was like the universe had turned on a spiritual faucet, and I couldn't shut it off—nor did I want to. As synchronicities go, I noticed sacred geometry symbols *everywhere* I went—as graffiti on a wall, on a poster at a store, or as the pattern on a rug. Before I left for Sedona, Nick told me that if I saw spiritual symbols that were out of the norm more than once and within a short period of time, then I had to pay attention to the message that might be surrounding them. Signs, he said, are the universe's way of communicating direction, guidance, answers, and validation that you're on a spiritual path.

From that point forward, I'd wake up at night with racing thoughts about the sacred geometry I saw and receive even more downloads of information about people and situations that I didn't know what to do with. I wasn't sure if what I was experiencing was real or if my imagination had run wild. For instance, I'd dream about writing a letter to my father, which I'd trust was an instruction from God; so when I'd wake up and do just that, I'd address all the feelings that I held inside—and feel so much better! I'd also dream of situations before they happened, like the time I saw myself house hunting in a strange neighborhood, and then the next day, I found myself looking at homes in the same setting as my dream. I might also dream of a phrase and then a few days later, someone would say it. I'd dream about dates as well, and when I'd type them into Google, I'd learn that an otherworldly event had happened on that day, perhaps a crop circle had been discovered. Collectively, these moments validated that a higher power was communicating with me and that I was being led down a special path. I reveled in my astonishing experiences and moved forward with faith and commitment.

HONING MY GIFTS

Four days after my trip to Sedona, I returned to Tucson, where I was living, and had an urge to do a healing on myself in a new way. Now when I say healing, I'm referring to an energetic clearing of any remaining negative and traumatic blocks that might have been holding me back in my life (I am *not* referring to healing health issues, which I didn't even realize was possible and came later in my spiritual growth). Though I'd visited a healer and cleared blocks on the vortex point, sometimes our energy fields require multiple clearings to fully cleanse, like when we are very ill or at the start of our spiritual journeys. I had no real awareness of this at the time—nobody had said as much—but I had a hunch that turned out to be true. I was also curious to find out if I could play with my energy, since others could read and manipulate it so well.

So I began to experiment with energy healing on myself. First, I ran my hand over my body and felt heat, tingling, and a magnetic sensation in areas where I was still blocked. I'd then sense what those blocks were connected to, what was causing them, and what would happen to me if I didn't fix them. To pull the block from my body, I'd gesture as if to scoop the area where I felt the toxin lived, remove it with my hand, then throw it into the center of the earth or up in the air, as if I were tossing a ball. I'd then ask God to fill me up with light and love and imagine replacing the block's vacancy with beautiful white light from the sky. Sometimes, I'd even put my hands in the sky and direct this energy's course to the top of my head. When I finished, I felt fully cleansed for the first time ever. I felt rejuvenated, clear, energized, and positive about my future. It felt like I'd fully detoxed, or finally eliminated, all the energetic toxins in my life.

Encouraged by this turn of events, I began doing healings on friends and family members who felt "off" or had things that weren't going their way but couldn't explain why. When this happens, there's a good chance the sensation is related to stuck energy. Some had unexplained anxiety or depression, others felt like they were going nowhere in their careers, and others had a traumatic past that they couldn't get over. Still others felt like they didn't have clarity on a topic or couldn't speak their truth; all of this led to feeling sad and heavy. And as I'd hoped, they all felt better after allowing me to heal them for anywhere between 20 minutes to an hour, depending on their baggage and what the universe would allow their bodies to release.

News spread about my abilities, and I began to quietly offer my skills to those in need—all via word of mouth from past clients. Because I was still working on my relationship and dating advice site, I did these healings for free—in fact, I gifted more than 10,000 sessions over a 10-year period. All my referrals and repeat clients came to me through friends, family, and even strangers I'd meet at marketing and business seminars that I attended for work.

My clients didn't always experience rainbows and butterflies when working with me. Sometimes their bodies physically purged the toxic energy that they needed to get rid of, which is fairly common among those who are heavily bogged down with stuck, toxic energy. My business partner Henry, for instance, had a lot of blockages in his stomach from feeling that he repeatedly gave away his power to others—in business, relationships, all of it. Energetically, the stomach is considered the center of will and power and located in the third/solar plexus chakra. Within an hour of removing Henry's blocks, he developed a stomachache and threw up! His energetic release created a physical response, and though I felt bad, it was a nice confirmation that my healing worked. Similarly, I once worked on a woman's inability to communicate her feelings on a heated subject with her spouse, which energetically affects the throat, or fifth chakra, and when she left me, she had a sore throat for days until the healing fully settled.

When I do a healing, I can absorb the other person's energy very easily. If I don't clear this energy, it can accumulate and cause me to be drained, have headaches, and generally feel terrible. I'll never forget the time I was in my parents' kitchen, and my right ankle began to hurt for no apparent reason. Five minutes later, my father came in from the garage in a grumpy mood. Energetically, the right side of the body is said to harbor male energy, and the pain was a clue that I was picking up on my dad's attitude; sure enough, on my drive home, the pain went away. I worked with a photographer whose knee hurt from a history of sports injuries. I didn't do a healing on her, but during our shoot, my kneecap felt like I'd injured it. I thought I'd sprained my knee in the gym, but after I left her, the pain went away.

If I ignore or resist these signals, other people's energy can become so intense that my body overheats. I have to take my socks off to release the trapped energy! The same thing can happen with my hands. Sometimes I soak my hands and feet in Epsom salt to detox them, and I always change my socks. At the end of a long day of serving others, I like to take a salt bath, turn off technology, connect with loved ones, play chess or *Ticket to Ride* with my son, or say a prayer to release the energy I've worked with that day. Sometimes simply being aware of it is enough to make the toxins dissipate.

A SPIRITUAL . . . WHAT?

I continued to conduct free healings on the West Coast for four years before moving to Sedona full time. Soon after, I was called home to California to help support my dad, who was struggling because of his business failings and unable to socially adjust to his life in the States.

While I was at my parents' house, the craziest thing started happening. Until that point, learning about healings and blockages had been my spiritual focus, and when I'd hear of something fun, I'd share it with my four sisters. Well, within a few days of spending time with them, they began to activate their own intuition and gifts, *just from being with me.* This was a remarkable next step in my energetic development. My sister Pia was able to physically and energetically heal through touch. Claudine became a channeler; in fact, the first time, she channeled an archangel who wanted to pass on timely business and relationship advice to me. My sister Liezl had premonitions that came true, and Elaine had ESP. Elaine and I liked to play a game where I'd hold up a playing card with the face turned away from her so she couldn't see it. I'd ask her to guess what it was, and she always got it right! Liezl also dreamed that our father was behind bars. She didn't think much of it, but six months later, my father had a fight with my mother, who felt threatened and called 911. Dad was detained overnight and bailed out the next day.

All of these activations happened in one weekend, but anytime I was with my siblings, we'd experiment and entertain ourselves with our collective energy. What a wild and amusing turn of events for a Filipino family raised to hide from such things! When a friend banged her knuckle in a stairwell, causing it to sprain and bruise, Pia put her hands over the injured hand and immediately heard a cracking noise. The pain was gone and the wound healed. This actually planted a seed in my mind that someday, I might be able to do physical healings as well as energetic ones. But I wouldn't be able to master that gift for another six years.

Though I recognized that I was somehow at the center of my sisters' spiritual activation, it would be another five years until I'd really recognize that in addition to healing, I could identify and set others' spiritual gifts and supernatural abilities into motion—be it as a healer, medium, psychic, and so on. As with my sisters, I could "turn on" their gifts through healings, so clients began calling me a Spiritual Activator. I was as surprised as anyone that I could do this, but I believe that my abilities were designed to work hand in hand. Energy healings clear blocks and encourage divine energy to flow, which helps ignite spiritual gifts.

NEW BEGINNINGS

I continued to do well as a consultant while doing healings on the side. I also got married, had a son named Braydon, but amicably separated from my first wife after five years. Our split drove me to visit Sedona yet again, this time to heal from the deep sadness, anger, heaviness, and guilt that was burdening my heart. It was no secret that my heart chakra had become really congested. Not only did I suffer because of my divorce, but I still anguished over my dad and childhood. I was desperate to fall in love with myself again. As I detoxed my heart, let's just say that I did a lot of crying—which was unusual for me, since I grew up having been taught not to express much emotion. But once I was free of my heart's entanglements, the universe returned me to myself. I wrote songs again and went on dates with myself to the movies and dinner. I practiced self-love, and it felt like coming home.

Just four days after I purged my lonely, congested, and toxic heart, my current wife, Mandy, floated into my orbit. I was scrolling Facebook and noticed her soulful face looking back at me in the "Friends You May Know" bar (yes...we met online). We had mutual friends, so I friended Mandy and watched a few of her videos about spirituality and wanting to change the world with love. I DM'ed her and said, "I love your message. But what are you selling?"

As it turned out, she was only making the videos to inspire others, but with my help, I had a feeling that we could spread her heartfelt message. Mandy and I messaged back and forth for a while, talking about everything from spirituality to channeling angels. Our friendship blossomed into dating, and we eventually moved to Sedona together, and then to Dallas.

Mandy was unlike anyone I'd ever met. She was a bright light of genuine integrity, a breath of fresh air. She was very purpose driven and didn't care so much about making money as she did about making an impact on the world, which she felt born to do. Most of all, Mandy did it all with love. This appealed to me, because my past had convinced me that leading with love wasn't the norm. I'll never forget how on one of our dates, I noticed that she was no longer walking beside me. When I turned around, Mandy was sitting on a bench with a homeless man, encouraging him to feel hope; and afterward, she gave him food and money. Mandy has such a deep and unshakeable love for others, reinforced by her connection to God. I found it all very attractive and inspiring. After feeling let down by so many people in my life, Mandy renewed my faith in humanity and showed me that there are good people in the world.

What's interesting is that shortly after meeting Mandy, my healing abilities shifted. For one, she taught me to infuse more love into my energy work. We also practiced how to channel on demand together, so I downloaded new and exciting messages about healing modalities from hidden archangels, learned how to use sacred geometry in new ways, and gathered fresh, general wisdom and practical advice to help me and my clients. Finally—and this was a biggie—in a meditation, my spirit guides gave me permission to practice physical healings. Until I met Mandy, I was told that I wasn't ready to do this, because I didn't have enough love in my heart. I had to let love flow through me and see the goodness in everyone to alleviate physical issues. Just being with Mandy inspired me to stop judging others and seeing them through society's eyes; I had to view them through God's eyes. To think that of the over 10,000 energy sessions I did, none were physical healings, because I didn't have enough love in my heart. It's rare to find a healer who possesses the right amount of unconditional love to restore health to a stranger.

Mandy launched her company Authentic Living, which mostly focused on teaching others how to raise their vibration and manifest their greatest desires, a few months after meeting me. She taught them how to move from abuse to happiness, from nine-to-five jobs to purpose work. I helped her from behind the scenes, offering strategy and marketing assistance. We were such great partners, in life and in the pursuit of our purpose work, that Mandy and I got married, gained custody of my son Braydon, and began building a life together. But it wasn't until Mandy was pregnant with our son Zion two years later that I decided to fully step into my healing business and become more invested in the company. I closed the marketing and consulting business that I'd launched to solely focus on teaching clients to become energy healers, activate their gifts, and pursue their purpose work.

When Mandy was pregnant with Zion, I thought a lot about what it meant to be a father. I wanted to be the best version of myself, so my children became my "why." I knew that I needed to shine my light full time and be seen—regardless of judgment—for my gifts, so that my sons would have a better life. Healing was such an intimate part of me, and choosing to do it full time definitely made me feel vulnerable. But I worked through it, because I didn't want my children to have a father who was afraid to be himself. At the heart of this was a worry that I'd repeat my own father's controlling, irrational, insecure, and overbearing tendencies. I didn't want to walk that familiar path. His suffering and unhappiness affected my sisters and me very deeply. I knew that I had to be a better role model for my family; I had to be more so my kids would be more.

SPREADING THE GEO LOVE

About a year into supporting Authentic Living from a marketing and business angle, I did my first official workshop teaching clients how to become healers, activate their gifts, and discover their purpose work. I believe so much in universal timing because I put the finishing touches on a bona fide program around the same time Mandy was pregnant. I felt ready to out myself as a healer and live that life fully.

I launched Geo Love Healing with the intention of giving as many people as possible the tools to master and clear their energy so they could feel centered and happy. I began with an initial, self-paced, 30-day program, and as my audience grew and went on to become energy healers with incredible stories of their own, I decided to offer certification programs. First, there's Geo 1, which teaches people to become healers, feel and remove energy in themselves and others, and heal others in person or remotely. Next comes Geo 2, which is a second level that teaches you to become a healer in group settings, plus learn more about your gifts, how to activate people's gifts, and how to use a healing modality called rainbow energy to clear physical conditions. Finally, there's Geo 3, an advanced energy course that explores soul traveling, generational and karmic healing, advanced techniques for severe physical conditions, how to channel, and how to play with time when conducting a healing. Collectively, all the programs are called Soul University.

The universe didn't give me access to sacred tools until my vibration matched that of the information I was meant to share. I had to be ready for it, or else I might misuse it. When creating my programs, I was always eager to learn the next tool, and waiting for it reminded me of waiting for the next season of my favorite TV show as a kid. I had to develop a lot of patience! Case in point: the lessons in this book's detox program took me nearly 10 years to learn and perfect!

Today, I lead sold-out events and teach packed, online sessions to clients all over the world. Our last event had 6,000 souls who paid to learn how to raise their vibration and live beautiful lives, and the next one we have planned should have 20,000 individuals registered.

I'm so excited to bring you my 15-day energy detox program. It's the culmination of everything I've studied, channeled, learned, taught, and practiced, and it has the power to transform your life. Clearing energy is integral to growth so that you awaken your gifts from an energetically clean slate and then pursue your purpose work for the highest good of all. A solid energetic detox is necessary, no matter where you are in your spiritual growth process.

Some of the techniques, like grounding and cutting cords, are inspired by what Christel and Nick taught me. I channel a lot of information too, like how to use sacred geometry and activate your and others' spiritual gifts.

Collectively, this simple, fun program will help you be and do your best. Like so many who've detoxed before you, you will glow from the inside out.

LET'S GET DETOXING!

In the coming chapters, I will help you detox your energy to remove the cumulative, negative effects of blocked energy on your physical, emotional, spiritual, and energetic bodies. Once you've eliminated the toxins that have built up in your auric field, you'll be poised to live your best life.

Much like a food or juice cleanse that jump-starts a healthy eating plan or purges your system of harmful toxins, you will cleanse your energetic body to activate your gifts and purpose work. This program will give you total peace, purpose, and clarity whenever you feel emotionally, physically, energetically, or spiritually bogged down. You'll learn to cleanse yourself from energetic blocks that slow down, dampen, or altogether stop your ability to thrive. I can't wait for you to harness the incredible energy that allows you to pursue all that you desire.

Chapter 2

WHY DO I NEED TO DETOX?

IF YOU COULD MAKE just one choice that would change the entire course of your life, would you do it? And if it took only 15 days to see results, wouldn't you wish you'd started yesterday? If this sounds like you, then I'm really glad you picked up this book. Because in less time than it takes to scroll through your Instagram each day, my detox will cleanse your system, connect you to your most authentic self, unveil your spiritual abilities, and spotlight your God-given purpose. But right now, I'll bet you have a lot of questions—for starters, why do I need to detox at all?

Energy detoxes are essential to living a peaceful, guided, and meaningful life. They allow you to clear as many energetic impediments, including energy blocks, as you can. This is part of an important process that helps you activate your innate gifts and pursue your purpose work from a purified state. Blocks can stop clear energy from flowing through you in ample form. Think of your energy as a river that courses through your body and auric field. When there are boulders, vegetation, and other obstructions in the water, a current won't move as quickly from its starting point, or watershed, to its finishing point. The water will take its time rippling, meandering, and pooling at a slower pace. It can become gross and contaminated. But when you detox your energy, you remove obstructions that let your fresh, energetic river move with ease. A natural, vibrational flow clears the way for divine intervention and energetic abundance to reach you and others.

Energy detoxes make sure that the wrong kind of energy doesn't plant itself in you like a seed; if you don't remove bad seeds from your energy field, they can take root and turn into a bigger issue. For example, a feeling of inadequacy from childhood trauma, over time, will grow branches that can lead to "rotten fruit" such as toxic romantic relationships, disrespectful family members, and the like. These scenarios can, in turn, trigger even deeper feelings of inadequacy. Most of us focus on plucking the rotten fruit from our lives, but we really need to focus on removing the root causes of our problems. Over the years, I've come to learn that the most troublesome roots come from that initial seed or energetic block. If you don't detox, which helps extract the root, you will energetically attract the wrong people, opportunities, and events into your life that reflect the low vibrational energy of your original issue. I'll explain more about how energy works in a bit, but for now, just know that like-energy attracts like-energy. So if harmful energy causes you to live on a vibration with harmful people and events, guess how your life will feel?

That's right—pretty toxic.

As I mentioned earlier, another fascinating result of detoxing is that it will reveal your spiritual abilities and guide you to your life's purpose. Believe it or not, we're all born with supernatural skills that we're meant to use for the highest good of all. You should never try accessing your gift on a lower, or pre-detox, frequency—if you do, you'll tap into darker or limited versions of your gift (more on this later). A person's gift reminds me of a fingerprint—no two people have the same one. And what's even cooler is that nobody's gift is more important than another's. Jane's healing ability isn't more essential than John's access to the Akashic Records (all the events, thoughts, and feelings that have occurred since the start of time, across all time and space). Humanity's supernatural skills are meant to work together to benefit the universe's collective energy. After your detox, you'll feel like "You 2.0"—and excited to share your gifts with the world.

Detoxing allows you to remove energy troubles so that you can thrive on a high vibration, make guided choices from that elevated state, and use your supernatural gifts to serve others. Your body will become a clear and clean vessel for the best energy to flow through it, which allows you to claim and pursue your purpose—plus, enjoy this planet to the fullest. Daily struggles will fall away as you receive new opportunities and encounter people who are peacefully like-minded and well-intentioned in their goals, just like you. Expect your authentic self to shine!

In this chapter, I'll introduce you to the importance of energy, the role that energy obstructions play in impeding free-will decisions, and how all of this relates to tapping into your gifts and guiding you to your fascinating purpose work. Every day, we make choices about how to protect and use our energy. If you create the intention to detox your field and hold yourself accountable for serving the highest good of all, that choice will shift the universe around you.

ENERGY: THE BASICS

Albert Einstein found that energy can be converted in form, but not created or destroyed. And since humans are fundamentally energetic, my detox is built to work with energy in all its expressions. There are different kinds of energy in the body, some of which are connected to the soul and some of which are products of the physical body. How we use, change, and develop our energy influences how our lives unfold in this lifetime and what happens to us while we're here on earth, and even when we die.

I don't want to spend too much time defining energy in a scientific language; I'd rather use the simple explanations and metaphors that I channel and teach in my workshops. With that said, all living things need energy to exist—from your deepest feelings to the plant sitting on your desk. As humans, we fuel our energy with our thoughts and emotions, which then dictate our behavior. This behavioral energy feeds future thoughts, emotions, and actions— and puts you on an energetic frequency where people and opportunities with similar energy exist. If a thought, emotion, or behavior leaves a very negative impression, it can form a block that grows when more negativity feeds it. This energetic muck, including blocks, lodges in various parts of your auric field and body—and requires cleansing before it wreaks havoc. Shifting your energy with a detox will shift your daily life along with it.

Energetic frequencies range from low to high and largely reflect the intensity of your emotional state. Low frequencies are fed by negative feelings like anger, sadness, and fear, whereas higher frequencies are powered by positive feelings like happiness, acceptance, and love. High vibrational energy feels so good to experience; it's light, calming, and comforting—the equivalent of a mushy, energetic hug. On the other hand, low vibrational energy feels dark, dense, and heavy. Imagine how you feel on a gloomy day, after a fight with your best friend, while battling a migraine . . . just plain awful. When you feel yourself slipping into low vibrational feelings, you should always aim to adjust your vibration to a higher emotional state. The energetically uplifting exercises I'll share in Part II of the book will help you achieve this. Think of changing vibrations like changing a TV channel. When you're on one channel, other channels still exist and send out energy; you've just chosen to live on a reality that exists on a certain channel. This dictates what you see, feel, and hear until you choose a different channel. Your energy interacts with the people, objects, land, food and other energetic influences that you experience. It doesn't need to last too long or be permanent. But doing the cleanse can quickly and efficiently change your energy channel.

By cleansing your energy, you'll come to live on a high vibration that will become your new normal and will feel incredibly natural to you. And because this energy supports you, you'll be less affected by random, negative events or energies. You can't live in a bubble and avoid all negativity, but you can raise your vibration to a point that you become unshakeable and unbreakable, mentally, emotionally, and energetically. You'll feel so protected because, unlike in the past, nothing can get to you, and lower vibes don't gain a foothold. For instance, visiting a house where a loved one recently died or overhearing nasty political pundits arguing on the news are scenarios that might ordinarily affect your vibration. But if you are operating from a high frequency, your lower vibration will be temporary and bounce back quickly. You might also feel your energy shift to a lower vibe while browsing an antique mall or crystal shop—where the store's relics carry all kinds of frequencies—but you won't feel their energetic imprints too heavily or for too long after leaving. You'll feel like yourself again, once outside their fields.

Not surprisingly, other people's energy can be contagious too. In the past, there were times that I'd talk to my mom on the phone before bed and she'd complain about money; the next morning, I'd wake up to calls from bill collectors and the bank for my own monetary shortcomings. But if I cleared my mom's energy after speaking to her, using the detox techniques in this book, then I not only felt lighter after our conversation, but the clearing created a space for simple answers to present themselves so I could help her too. Best of all, rather than have creditors call, I might receive an e-mail about a lucrative project. The universe would present positive opportunities before problems could even surface.

A lot of spiritual experts like to talk about using positive language and avoiding negative language to shift or raise your vibration. But when it comes to the words that tumble off your tongue, I feel it's their intention and emotional intensity that most affect your frequency. Sincerity and potency feed energy like fertilizer to a garden. When you're ill, for example, you can't expect to be healed if you push yourself to talk about gratitude and miracles with a resentful or heavy heart. You must speak or pray for your desires with positive sincerity and enthusiasm to give it the energetic punch that shifts frequencies. This *oomph* is more powerful than robotically reciting affirmations, mantras, or rote prayers many times in a row too.

Making every effort to live on a high frequency will keep your fields clear and fewer blocks from forming, so you'll create a free-flowing pathway for the most awesome energy. This makes it easier to design the life you want, because you'll have guided, divine assistance from the universe and co-create from a heart space aligned with the universe's highest good.

CLEARING THE BUILDING BLOCKS OF CHAOS

When it comes to energetic impediments that require clearing, there's the gross, low vibrational energy that lingers in your auric field, chakras, and physical body—and then there are the bona fide blocks that form when this energy accumulates. Energetic blocks are powerful and can stop heartfelt intentions and passionate goals from occurring. This is because blocks have negative beliefs, emotions, and sometimes even physical conditions attached to them, which will hold you back in the real world. It's like trying to drive a car with the handbrake on. Blocks occur when low frequency feelings like fear, guilt, anger, and inadequacy make their way into your aura, chakras, or physical being. When this happens, it's not enough to force yourself to be positive or remind yourself that you're happy or loved. Your energy is a frequency lodged within you, and when you're genuinely vibrating low, blocks need to be conscientiously removed.

Most energetic blocks begin in your auric field, which I consider the skin of your energetic body. If a block goes deeper, caused by personal and energetic triggers, it will penetrate one or more of the eight chakras (there are typically seven, but I'll share one more). Your chakras stretch from the base of your spine to the top of your head. They are the root chakra (at the base of the spine), sacral chakra (lower abdomen), solar plexus chakra (upper abdomen/ stomach area), heart chakra (center of chest, just above the heart), throat chakra (throat), ear chakra (inside your ears), third eye chakra (forehead, between the eyes), and crown chakra (very top of the head). As a side note, you also have energy centers in your hands, feet, and throughout your body. Finally, if a block isn't cleared for a while, it will begin to affect the physical body, including injury to your immune and nervous systems, muscles, tissues, and organs; nasty energy can even bury itself deep in your DNA—or even deeper, in a fetus's energetic field or body, while its mother is pregnant. Energetic blocks, then, can become a generational trait, just like tiny ears or big blue eyes.

One of your detox goals is to clear all your blocks at their roots, but this may not happen in one try. *This has nothing to do with you.* That's right: your ability to fully remove a block doesn't wholly depend on you or your abilities. Remember, when you work to remove an energetic block, God controls how much of this block can be released at that time, based on that which is in the highest good for all. The rate at which your block clears may be linked to frequency, learning a lesson first, or a divine timeline you won't know until the block is gone and you can connect the dots in retrospect. That's the funny thing about cleansing. After chipping away at a block, you might experience the most amazing miracle you've ever known—or simply feel a little better than before. Like a flower that blooms when it's ready, everything happens in its own divine and perfect time.

The best way that I can describe a block's configuration is by illustrating what I sense and feel whenever I do a healing, clearing, or activation session on someone. Here, I like to hold my hand about three or four inches away from a person's skin, which is where a block would live in their auric field, and then I move my hand around the outline of their body. This is something I also do remotely, most of the time as well. You don't have to be in front of a person physically to be able to work on their energetic body. I pay attention to each of their eight chakras as I do this. If there's a block in your aura, any of the chakras, or anywhere in the physical body, my hands will burn or feel a kind of tension, as if a magnet is pushing them away. I get intuitive hits about where blocks are located too. Sometimes I sense the block's texture, which feels like a hot, heavy, and slimy ball. I can also tell when the block has deep roots, like a thicket of weeds that beg to be chopped as if my hand were a Weedwhacker, or pulled out using a similar motion to pulling weeds, or swept up similarly to a broom cleaning out debris and dirt. Some healers can look at a person and see a color or goo in a blocked area. They might also feel the block in their own body, which happens to me too. Honestly, most block forms differ, depending on the person, block, and healer's perception. An intense block rooted in decades of generational trauma can have an energetic signature I've never encountered, since it's created by the person I'm healing, those attached to the block, and all the generational energy that formed the block. I'll discuss generational blocks more deeply later in the chapter. For now, know that most blocks are unique since the energy that creates them is so personal.

Energetic blocks slow down, dampen, or stop your ability to be the best version of you. Your soul's internal guidance system gets muted when your body is riddled with toxic blocks, and you can't make the wisest decisions for yourself or those who depend on you. At your most natural state, in which filtered energy flows freely through you, clarity and direction are a given. You feel led to use your supernatural gifts for the highest good. Your high energy keeps you aligned with your higher power and feeling healthy in various ways.

If blocks get in the way of shining your light—in other words, aligning with your truest nature, as God intended for you to live—it's the energetic equivalent of stuffing yourself with junk food and expecting to feel like a well-nourished triathlete. Blocks affect you on all levels—physical, spiritual, and emotional. They can initiate physical illness, pain, fatigue, and headaches. You can also feel spiritually affected with dark, intuitive dreams about a crime or traumatic memory—even feel lost or abandoned by God and his archangels. Emotionally, you could feel on the verge of a breakdown, crying at the drop of a hat. In all cases, blocks make you feel like your soul is screaming out that something is very wrong, but you can't pinpoint the problem or fix it. You feel glued in place and don't understand why so many things, in every aspect of your life, are going sideways. The more blocks you accumulate, the harder it becomes to recognize yourself, since you're so busy trying to feel normal every day. You tread water to survive, despite the chaos in your personal and professional lives. Deals fall through at work, relationships struggle, appliances break—any and all impediments to a pleasant day fall down around you. These are all clues that the universe is showing you that your current reality is being highly compromised by the blocks in your life.

BAD THINGS COME IN THREES

There are three categories of energy blocks that I typically see in clients prior to a detox. These are the biggies that need to be cleared for optimal physical and mental health as well as to gain access to spiritual gifts. They are the most common and destructive. They're what God's shown me are crucial to detoxing energetic, spiritual, and physical bodies.

The first blocks I often see are called Traumatic Blocks, and they come from past events that create emotionally and energetically toxic energy that lodge itself in your auric field and physical body, often due to abandonment, abuse, loss, grief, bad relationships, and the like. These kinds of blocks manifest as feelings of hurt, shame, anger, betrayal, uselessness, and discord. Often, this painful experience works its way into your belief system, becomes the story you tell yourself and others—and ultimately, controls your identity. All of this causes you to unconsciously reenact the same problem, over and over. The emotional, mental, and behavioral patterns reinforce the energy block, and in your 3-D life, make you feel stuck and keep you from moving forward.

Second are Environmental Blocks. You take on these blocks empathetically, when you absorb the energy of your environment or those in either your immediate space (like in a crowded room) or greater life (a loved one in a bad mood). Before you know it, you might feel a headache or unshakeable thought or feeling, like anxiousness, guilt, or overwhelm. You know this is an Environmental Block and not an unconscious block that you've created, because it will come on suddenly, be the opposite of what you were previously feeling at that moment, and you won't be able to figure out its genesis. At first, you might think you caused the block, but with enough digging, you might realize that it didn't start with you. So often, we experience thoughts, emotions, and physical ailments that we believe are ours to solve, but they're coming from someone or somewhere else. Clearing Environmental Blocks helps you (and those around you) to function better.

The third category are Familial Blocks, which includes both Generational Blocks and Gestational Blocks. When a block gets imprinted on our bodies at a cellular level—running as deep as our DNA—and can be passed down from one generation to the next, this is called a Generational Block. Clients with these issues are tempted to repeat negative patterns, both conscious and subconscious, that were ingrained in them by their moms and grandmothers, fathers and grandfathers. For instance, when my wife's mom was pregnant with her, she lost her home after a divorce and was low on money. So, when Mandy was pregnant with Zion, she began to feel overwhelming and unfounded fears about losing *our* home and having money problems too. This made no logical sense at the time because we were doing well. It was, however, a major clue to knowing that Mandy had Generational Blocks passed down from her mother's painful experience to her. Another example is that my grandfather, father, and I all had the same inexplicable fear of needles as children. The emotionally charged response imprinted itself on me and my elders' energy fields. It may seem from this example that Generational Blocks can be learned, but this isn't the case. It is an energetic transference. Real-life events trigger the energy, emotions, and memories that are stored in your cells. Another example of how memories, which have energy, can be stored in your body's cells are patients who get organ transplants. Suddenly, they crave food they've never liked, have new hobbies, and watch shows they previously hated because these were all habits of the organ donor.

Unlike Generational Blocks, Gestational Blocks occur only during the nine months that a child is in its mother's womb. Since every thought and trauma has an energetic frequency, these can create Gestational Blocks through energetic channels while the baby shares its mother's body. The mom's beliefs, emotions, and experiences transfer to the child—who then grows up and genetically passes this down to *their* kids via Generational or Gestational Blocks. This might happen if your mom was ill during her pregnancy or if a gestational carrier, or surrogate mother, emotionally struggles with having to detach from the infant she's carrying. I've also seen it in clients when a mother has a block in her heart from feeling unsupported by her partner during pregnancy or when a mother is in an abusive relationship or takes drugs while she's pregnant. The child then develops the same blocks (mistrusting men, attachment issues, and so on) that their mother had while carrying them. On the other hand, if a terrible event occurs during pregnancy—say, the mother contracts a life-threatening disease—but trusts her doctor and feels no fear, anger, or other negative emotion around this diagnosis, no block will form. Feeling confident about her health does not create a negative, emotional response, so even though the illness itself is scary and dangerous, it will not leave a Gestational Block on the baby.

INTERNAL VERSUS EXTERNAL INFLUENCES

Any block you encounter will be encouraged by both internal and external influences—and I want to draw your attention to these for a few reasons. First, it's important to be aware of what components build your blocks and then amplify them so you can do your best to avoid them in the future. Oftentimes, simply being aware of what causes and feeds your blocks is enough to initiate an energy shift. The act of knowing lifts you out of negative states like denial and frustration and into more neutral or positive frequencies. This awareness can act as a stepping stone toward a higher vibration and more positive feelings like gratitude, forgiveness, and love. If you ride the emotional and energetic momentum, you may feel encouraged to cleanse the block. Now sometimes, energy work is *not* enough to remove a block; you may need to combine it with emotional work to fully release its attachment. I've included easy, therapeutic exercises in Part II of this book, so you'll know where and when in the detox process to do them.

Internal influences are the easiest to control. I don't mean that these are simple to excavate, because they're not; internal influences just live inside of you, so with enough insight, you can make sense of them and initiate change. Internal factors tend to live deep inside your psyche, and you'll know you've hit on a good one because your self-protective mind might want to ignore it. We can create internal influences that feed blocks at any point in our lives, though in my clients, trauma-related triggers tend to develop during childhood. Nonetheless, internal influences include the way you emotionally process and feel about relationships with your friends, peers, family, partner, and so on. They revolve around feelings that are painful and difficult to digest, like shame, fear, and regret. All the choices you make count as internal influences too, since decision-making is a mental process. It takes courage, speaking your truth, and moving out of your comfort zone to conquer blocks fed by internal factors. Breaking free of these detrimental internal influences helps you get to the core of a block faster than dealing with an external factor that feeds a block.

External influences that feed blocks can be harder to control, mainly because they involve people as well as circumstances that don't live within you. Negative external factors that feed blocks and jar your energy include things that are *done or said to you* by family, a spouse, colleagues—plus, external energy-manglers like electromagnetic fields (EMFs), pollution, electrical sources, the land you live on, your proximity to power lines, the global climate, and even junk food. Since you often can't predict when an external influence will throw off your peace, a honking horn on the freeway or grumpy call from Dad can really flip your energy on its head. You can't prepare for this assault, so the best you can do is sustain a high vibration and hope it doesn't stick.

Often blocks are caused by a messy soup of internal and external influences—which is one reason bad energy can be tough to untangle. My client Debra came to me when her $20 million healthcare company was underperforming, her mind felt cluttered with negative self-talk, and she desperately craved a kind and loving boyfriend. To look at Debra, you'd think she had it all—great business, fancy house, beautiful appearance. But Debra was troubled at heart. She also suffered from debilitating migraines, causing her to spend hours curled up on any floor in the darkest room she could find. Her energy blocks were in her aura, chakras, and body.

After scanning Debra's body and tapping into my intuition, I recognized that the root of her problems was her toxic father, an external influence she couldn't shake. Her father cheated on and divorced Debra's mother when Debra was young; he belittled and emotionally abused Debra all her life. This caused Debra to feel tremendous guilt and shame over most decisions she made. Debra chose partners who reminded her of her father because his behavior was familiar. She even hired employees that she felt her father would like, even though he didn't work at her company or even in the same field. It's no surprise that this made Debra's professional environment a nightmare. Though Debra consistently made poor choices based on her past, the core of her block was external since her father's energy was indominable and bullying. What's amazing is that Debra put a lot of effort into therapy for years, working with a life coach, and attending many weeklong spiritual retreats— yet her energy remained a problem.

Debra was so desperate for help that my wife and I cleared our schedules for the day to work solely on her. I worked with Debra to remove her energetic blocks using techniques I've included in the book. Mandy, who has a more therapeutic background, taught Debra about boundaries, positive self-talk, and how to emotionally free herself from her father's grip. A few months after she returned home, Debra received an offer to buy her business and met a doting, successful, and heartfelt man that she's still dating today—a series of events that might have otherwise taken her years, or even decades, to achieve. She detoxes every few months and practices many of the techniques in this book as part of her daily meditation practice. She feels calm, happy, fulfilled—and best of all, free of her father's control. I'm incredibly proud of Debra's dramatic turnaround, which occurred in such a short time.

YOUR GIFTS MAY NOT SURPRISE YOU

When you detox, you not only feel better, but you clear an energetic pathway for your spiritual gifts and purpose work to emerge. Some clients recognize their primary gift immediately, others have always known what it is, and still others have spent their lifetime running away from their abilities. It's common to feel completely clueless about your gift too. No matter what your situation, your primary gift will kick down your spiritual door around Day 5 or 7 of the detox. You'll notice that a gift is igniting within you, because you'll feel overcome by its exciting traits. You might have vivid dreams that you can't turn off, become sensitive to other people's emotions and thoughts, or feel an insatiable heat in your arms and hands if you're a healer. Forthcoming energy can also present as anxiety, headaches, dizziness, or pressure in your head, which are never fun but still a relevant clue that your gifts are primed to surface. They are signs that the universe is calling you to release that energy via your gift.

Chances are, your spiritual gift has always been part of you, likely revealing itself a little at a time, but your mind and soul simply didn't know how to turn these random skills into spiritual purpose work. One year, we donated our retreat center to our town's sheriff, who threw a Christmas party for his department. That night, I had a fascinating conversation with one of his top detectives named John, a real whiz at solving crimes. He asked what I did for a living, and in no time, we were talking chakras, crystals, and spirituality—subjects that were all new to him. I went on to explain how I'd had past clients who were also detectives, and they used their spiritual gifts to enhance their job performance. John was flabbergasted. I explained how one cop in a drug enforcement unit could literally taste the drug that a victim had OD'd on, and another officer could touch evidence and instinctively know how it related to his case. When I mentioned a third detective who often heard a voice guiding his work, John's eyes widened. "I've heard that voice too!" he exclaimed. John said that one time, he was called to the scene where a man robbed a liquor store, and when John went to his house to arrest him, John heard a voice whisper, "Duck!"— so he did. Not even seconds later, a bullet grazed the top of John's head, nearly killing him. John didn't know where the voice came from, so I taught him about spiritual guidance, gifts, and the importance of detoxing to keep divine channels open for the highest good. Our conversation led to John opening his third eye even more and piqued his curiosity so much that we began working together so that I could teach him how to detox and regularly lean on his gifts. Recently, John shared that he just received a promotion at work and is in the process of writing a book and TV script about his journey.

If you try to access your gifts pre-detox, you may find, like some clients, that your energy isn't clear enough for a positive result. For example, if you haven't worked on issues around your negativity, fear, and anger in a cleanse, and then open your third eye, your abilities can feel draining. You'll also tune in to other negative events—because again, like attracts like. If your gift shows you to be an innate channeler and you haven't detoxed, you will have access to the spirit world, but you'll likely connect to negative and dark entities instead of archangels and other elevated souls that walk in the light. I had a client named Disha who was always visited by angry, dark entities— often in bed or in the shower. She unknowingly fed this heavy energy by watching scary movies, going to corner psychics who insisted that bad spirits were attached to her, and having frequent arguments with her family. Disha felt like she was losing grip on reality and couldn't seem to escape these constant, ghostly hauntings. This entire constellation of torment contributed to putting Disha on a very low frequency where only negative souls and experiences were available to her. When I taught Disha how to clear her energy, she said she slept peacefully for the first time in a year. After practicing additional detox steps at home, Disha reported that she no longer had any scary encounters at all. Her demons were slayed.

Gifts can evolve and be combined, but if you're not careful, they can also disappear. All the spiritual work we do is meant to align, but it can be hard to see the forest for the trees. I know a healer who did a clearing on a psychic and had a series of validating visions during the experience. This encouraged the healer, and made her feel more confident about her gift, prompting her to help more people than before. That said, I've also seen clients gain tremendous abilities from a detox but, after a cascade of negative experiences, have their energy drop. This lower vibration then causes their abilities to decrease, become blocked in certain ways, or disappear altogether. The latter is common if your ego gets involved. The universe will turn off your gifts like a light, and you'll completely lose the spiritual abilities you once had.

UNEXPECTED REWARDS

One of my favorite parts of detoxing is when clients notice helpful, small changes that fall outside the categories of gifts and purpose work; here, the gifts simply enhance their life and validate that a protective higher power is steering them in the right direction. This happens because you're graduating to different realities and frequencies. It may become easier to sense direction, protection, and guidance, even with daily tasks. You might have a gut feeling about whether to take a job, forgo a trip, buy a book, or take a different route to work. You might also find that relationships, home, sleep, health, job, and finances change for the better. And though healing physical illness is not our goal with an energy detox, bodily ailments can improve or disappear completely—I've seen it with my own eyes. Sometimes, when you remove blocks from your energetic body, you can remove energy related to an illness. So if you aim to clear a block in your heart, it doesn't matter if it's caused by disease or emotional pain from a breakup; your detox clears the energy, regardless. In every situation, when you're doing a general detox, have faith that you're removing everything that needs to be healed— in that moment in time, for the highest good of all. God doesn't remove what you *want*, but what you *need* to let your life flow. God's work may not make sense at the time, but trust the process. Soon, you'll see how the all-knowing universe rearranged your life to allow your gifts and purpose to change your world.

More Resources and Free Downloads

I've put together a powerful video that goes over energy blocks in more detail, and more importantly, what you can do to release the blocks right now so you can move forward to the next chapter of your life, empowered, free, and happy. Download the video for free here: www.SpiritualActivator.com/energyblocks

---

PART II

YOUR 15-DAY PLAN

Chapter 3

DAYS 1–3: PROTECT YOUR ENERGY

THE INITIAL STEP OF your energetic detox is to spend the first three days of the program learning to protect the energy in your body and auric field. This will give your mind a rest and buffer your vibration from the infiltration of any new, energetic burdens. It is similar to a food detox where you initially eliminate harmful foods from your diet and start eating foods that are easy to digest and assimilate as your system cleanses and heals. Just as these new and healthier foods offer protection from additional toxins entering your physical body, the spiritual safeguarding techniques that I'll teach you in this chapter will shield you from energetic contaminants.

Why worry about spiritual protection at all? As we've discussed, every day you face a minefield of negativity that influences the energy inside and outside your body. And without protection, the energy in your environment, including from people and other factors, affects your frequency—and not always in the best way. Protection can make the difference between a day you enjoy and one that completely debilitates you. It's this dark and funky negative energy that develops and feeds blocks. So if you spend significant time with a toxic friend or partner, without daily protection, their energy will deeply engage with yours and potentially affect your thoughts and feelings, which can skew your internal energy too. So before you do anything else, you must master how to protect your body from external, negative energy that pours out from friends, colleagues, family members, Wi-Fi, and other powerful sources. These techniques will help keep your internal energy safe too. After all, negative energy inside your body can cause thoughts and emotions that feed the choices you make and how you process your feelings. We'll address how to get rid of these toxins in the next chapter about deeper cleansing.

You might be surprised to realize the extent to which negative external energy not only exists around and within you but also how it can impact your physical and mental health. This is why creating effective protection is so imperative. Negative influences are everywhere. Let's use the example of a work commute. On your way to the office, you might interact with a grumpy train conductor, absorb a mix of overwhelmed, annoyed, and bitter vibrations from other commuters, soak up toxic energy from the overhead wires that power the train, feel jostled and flustered by rushed workers on your way out the door, navigate a busy street with self-centered pedestrians, hear a cacophony of honking horns and sirens on your smog-filled walk to work, and then finally—finally!—settle into a meeting where you're met by colleagues full of anxiety and stress. See where I'm going with this? Though you've barely started your day, your energy has already fought off countless frequencies that, without spiritual protection, could send your own energy on a real rollercoaster. Without protection, a necessary daily event like commuting can initiate or feed a chronic state of misery.

If you create and wear the type of energetic shield that you'll learn to build in this chapter, I guarantee that your energy will be fully protected and, best of all, help you focus on and support positive ambitions like building a business, stepping into your purpose work, finding a new home, experiencing optimum wellness, growing your family—or simply feeling at peace. Anger, shame, regret, and other negative feelings can intensely lodge themselves in your energetic field and chakras too, since they create upsetting thoughts that carry low energy. But to clear this energy you must strategically release the pain associated with it and raise your vibration, which you'll learn about in the next chapter.

In this chapter, we'll explore why protection is essential, specific techniques to use for protection, and remarkable stories about clients whose lives were changed because they learned how to protect themselves as an important first step to energy detoxing.

WHEN TO BUILD PROTECTION

There are three protection tools that I use to guard energy. I'd like you to try one a day and couple it with the tool(s) from the prior day. I call this, layering. Your protection shield will layer (1) the power of intention, (2) sacred geometry, and (3) color and light therapy to form an energetic shield that protects you from outside negativity. Figuring out which combination of techniques works best is a personal, intuitive, trial-and-error process with no wrong answers. At the end of the three days, you'll have a few options that make you feel more confident with facing negative vibrations. Do this daily, first thing in the morning, so that you can get used to what it feels like to start your day with clarity, energy, peace, and protection.

TOOL #1: INTENTION

The first mode of protection is intention, which you'll focus on during Day 1. When you set an intention, you're asking the universe for your request to materialize in the real world and at a high frequency. I like to make sure there are three parts to all intentions: what you want, what you want to remove, and what you'd like to experience throughout the day. To create an intention, close your eyes, take a deep breath, and say something like this aloud, "I set the intention that I be protected from negative energy. I want to filter out whatever is not for the highest good. Please send me love-based energy to combat any negativity I might come across today." Reciting this first thing in the morning or before you step into a situation that may affect you (being in a crowded area or a meeting with someone you know who has a history of affecting or draining your energy) not only protects you for the entire day, but it also establishes a habit that gets your morning off on the right foot.

As you move through Day 1 with intentional protection, heighten your awareness of what's happening around you. You may notice surprising but welcome synchronicities such as accidentally sleeping in but later finding out that you avoided an accident on your way to work, or missing a dentist's appointment only to find out later that your favorite hygienist was on vacation. Frustrating events might also surface, like a lucrative project falling through or an upsetting e-mail—in cases like these, you must trust that God has better plans for you that sync up with your soon-to-be clear, energetic state. A lot of times we don't realize that things are truly happening for us, and what seems like a "failure" or "punishment" is actually the best thing for us to experience at the moment. For example, let's say you want to write a book, and you get rejected by a book publisher. In that moment, it may feel like rejection but what if it happened because in 30 days another publisher was going make an offer even beyond what you hoped for. A lot of times, if we just stretch the time frame we look at things, we'd realize that life truly is happening for us even if it doesn't feel like it.

Though your initial intention is enough to protect you throughout the day and help you stand in your power, you can also add a second or third during precarious situations. For instance, if you're headed into an important business lunch, you could say, "God, please fill me with love, courage, and strength. Remove all negative and lower-level energies during this lunch. I want to experience only positive emotions for the highest good of all." You can even attach a time frame to your request—and since you've already set an intention for the day, this can be as short as you wish. So if spying a gaggle of mean moms during the school drop-off makes your stomach turn, try stating, "For the next hour, please help me experience friendliness, joy, and peace—and protect me from anyone or anything that could lower or throw off my energy, for the highest good of all." If I know I'm headed to a potentially contentious family dinner or a crowded mall for holiday shopping, I say this intention, "God, please protect me from all toxic, fear-based, negative energy for the next twelve hours"—and it does the trick. As you become more comfortable with establishing this type of protection, creating time-based intentions is a fun exercise to try because you can track the efficiency of your protection in real time. You'll either sense the subtle calm that comes with the fulfillment of an intention—or you won't, and you can reword it and try again. I loved doing this when I was first learning protection, because it boosted my confidence in the process. Eventually, you may need only one intention statement to cover you for the day or during a difficult moment.

By now, I'm sure you've noticed that setting an intention sounds a lot like saying a prayer. That's because the energy you put forth in an intention statement is why prayer works. When a positive intention genuinely comes from your heart, which has a larger energetic field than even your brain, you're making a request with deep emotion that elevates your vibration. And when you invoke a higher power or God to fulfill your request, it puts you in the dynamic vibration of trust that can set wheels in motion. Sincere and honest intention statements imply that you know you're co-creating with a higher power and handing over protection to God, who has the intelligence and capability to fulfill a request. You trust that God will get the job done.

TOOL #2: SACRED GEOMETRY

On Day 2 of your cleanse, you'll add sacred geometry to your protection shield. Sacred geometry attaches symbolic and sacred meaning to certain geometric shapes. There are countless types of sacred geometry at your disposal, so I suggest that you play around with three shapes to start. My personal favorites are the three-dimensional pyramid, sphere, and spiral—they're the most common symbols found in nature and architecture, plus they're also very effective.

If these shapes don't resonate, there are many others to use. They include stars, pyramids, flowers, octagons, spirals, lattices, tunnels, funnels, honeycombs, cobwebs, triangles, gardens, pentagons, tetrahedrons, the Hand of Fatima (popular in Middle Eastern cultures), and the Tibetan Knot (you may have seen this on bracelets, jewelry, and rugs). These sacred shapes can be found in and on Egyptian pyramids, seashells, leaves, the Star of David, art, snowflakes, architecture, temples, and churches. Even your DNA is shaped like a ladder—AKA, a three-dimensional double helix.

Nearly all human cultures reference sacred geometry in some way, as far back as ancient rock carvings and cave paintings. Greek and Roman philosophers theorized that sacred geometry is the blueprint for life and believed that God's geometric plan formed the basis of all matter.

Specific geometric shapes were even said to have symbolic or spiritual meanings. In shamanistic traditions, sacred geometry conveys messages from the spirit world, and there are many ancient tales whose authors claim that if you put fresh fruit inside Egyptian pyramids, it slows their decay.

More recently, a researcher named Bill Kerell, who conducts experiments using pyramids and brine shrimp, found that the shrimp typically live six to seven weeks, but under a pyramid, they can live for over a year. He's also noted that shrimp grow three times larger than their normal size in these spaces. And in one Canadian hospital study conducted in a burn ward, doctors placed patients under a pyramid-shaped structure for a few minutes and found this reduced patients' pain and burns healed much faster. I believe this is because sacred geometry protects what's inside, above, around, and beneath it, since they hold an astounding energy for good. You can achieve similar benefits by purchasing a pyramid-shaped bed, wearing a pyramid-shaped hat (my wife and I do this around the house!), or sleeping with a small copper pyramid under the bed. Many EMF shields that you can buy online are shaped like pyramids too.

Sacred geometry symbols have literally appeared in my visions and dreams, and I've used them to protect myself and heal others, since they're such a natural part of our universe. Some scientists argue that seeing these shapes may be more of an optical illusion than a spiritual phenomenon. We know that living organisms and natural objects adhere to geometric and mathematical constants like Phi, or the golden ratio (for example, snowflakes, nautilus shells, and flowers). Yet when people report seeing them while on hallucinogenic drugs, during near-death experiences, after sensory deprivation or a traumatic brain injury, with epilepsy or schizophrenia, and when applying pressure to the eyeballs, neuroscientists raise an eyebrow. They say that sacred geometry shapes are simply how our brains' visual cortex maps and interprets the world under certain conditions.

At the end of the day, why does sacred geometry have to be one or the other—scientific fact or spiritual anomaly? These geometric patterns make up our reality and certain conditions make it possible to see them. How many times have you heard about someone who experienced a neurological infection or car accident—and then suddenly became wildly intuitive? Or take author Jason Padgett, who explains in his memoir *Struck by Genius*, that he became a mathematical genius after a violent mugging. The incident changed how Jason's brain functions. He now sees crystalline patterns when water pours from the faucet, numbers that reference geometric shapes, and fractal patterns on tree branches, among other oddities. The way Jason now interprets the world reveals the mathematic designs hidden in the objects around us.

I've seen sacred geometry shapes access, maintain, and amplify energy—especially when little else works for protection or even healing. Our bodies naturally respond to sacred geometry because it's inside and around all of us. Sacred geometry is the language of God, since it's in the cosmos—and more specifically, in nature. At a workshop that I led with Mandy, many of the students came to work through trauma. Our student Julia was highly intuitive but had never acknowledged that gift and had never detoxed her energy. As a result, her unprotected empathic gift was physically debilitating. She was hypersensitive to environmental energy, so as each attendee shared their tragic story, Julia became increasingly ill with nausea, migraines, shortness of breath, and a ringing in her ears. Midway through, she was lying on the floor, covering her face with a shawl. I pulled Julia out of the event and began to teach her how to protect herself. We tried pairing intention statements with color therapy, but it wasn't until we used sacred geometry that her body calmed down. Ultimately, protecting Julia by having her envisioning a pyramid with a sphere on top was the shape combination that allowed her to function.

When the universe first began sending me sacred geometry, I wasn't in an altered state. I didn't take drugs or have a brain injury. When I opened myself up on that Arizona vortex, these amazing shapes simply started coming to me at random times—mostly during the night as well as during or after a healing. Sometimes when I looked at an object, much like Jason Padgett, I'd see the geometric symbols that made it up. For a good seven months, the universe bombarded me with sacred geometry. This tapered off but then they began appearing intermittently during dreams that woke me at 3 A.M. The time isn't a coincidence, as 3 to 4 A.M. is often called "the holy hour"; it's when the barrier between the spiritual and physical realms is thinnest. Every time sacred symbols appeared to me, I'd scramble to find a pen and paper to draw the shapes so I wouldn't forget them. I began teaching them as shield tools.

So on Day 2 when you're layering intentions with sacred geometry, I'd like you to begin with a quick statement that focuses on finding the right shape for you. While the intention will be focused on the outcome that is desired, the shape holds the energy and intention together so it's even more powerful and has a container. You could say, "Please help me find the best shape for protection." Then imagine yourself inside a few different shape configurations, almost like a force field, and try to experience these symbols with all five senses. Deep engagement will help the shape work its powerful magic. Finally, choose only one that's an intuitive fit.

Now that you can imagine yourself surrounded by your sacred geometry symbol, play with its size and texture. Make the shape as big or small as you'd like depending on the environment you're in. For some, visualizing the shape works, while others benefit from simply setting the intention to be protected by the shape. Use whichever symbol resonates for protection, for as long as it suits you. You don't need to be married to this shape forever. Give it a go for a few weeks, then try another shape if you'd like. Choosing protection is an intuitive process of trial and error, and there are no wrong choices.

TOOL #3: COLOR AND LIGHT THERAPY

To use color for protection, first set an intention like, "Please help me find the color that will protect me from negative energy," and then imagine yourself in your sacred geometry shape. Different colors resonate with different people. During workshops, I typically suggest you first tap into the energy of gold, and if that's not a fit, play with colors like white, purple, and green (I don't know if there's a divine reason for this; they're just the most effective). Now, don't beat yourself up if you can't visualize the color. Some people, as weird as it sounds, can hear the color, feel the color, and some don't do this part of the process at all. Once you've connected with a color, imagine it streaming down from the heavens to fill up your shape. If the color fills your body too, that's fine, but it's not a must. Think of the geometric shape as a container that holds the light intact. At this point, you should feel deeply connected to your color. But if the color doesn't feel right, just choose another. Sometimes, clients like to use multiple colors. Play with your color(s). Make it darker, lighter, brighter, denser, and more or less dynamic in your mind. Decide which "texture" this light or color is. Some clients transform the color from a beaming light into a smooth liquid inside their symbol, like a lava lamp. Experiment until the intensity of the color reaches its max; if you feel only moderately affected, keep pouring the light in. You've reached your goal when you feel energized, peaceful, calm, or tingly, or your instincts tell you that you've hit your peak—this varies for each person. Set an intention for the day, visualize yourself in sacred geometry, bask in your color—and your shield is complete!

CHOOSE THE BEST COMBO FOR YOU

Though using these three components to form your protection shield might seem like overkill, you never know when you're about to enter an intense situation, have a fight with a friend, or consume entertainment or social media that elicits a strong emotional response. Building a shield is like constructing your own Fort Knox. Imagining yourself inside your shield lets you walk through the world in your own energy—which will soon be detoxed, clear, and pure. Once you're comfortable with your mega-shield, you may decide to pare back. Perhaps an intention statement works on its own, or sacred geometry plus light. Finding the most effective tools to shield you from environmental energy is a very personal, intuitive choice.

You can be creative with the images that make you feel safe. I've had clients set intentions and then visualize themselves surrounded by light-beaming flowers or a pink star. Some imagine themselves in the center of a whirlwind that's so powerful that it pulls negative energies from their bodies and casts them off as they spin inside it. Others like to layer systems of protection where one bubble of light spins in one direction, another bubble of light spins in another, and a pyramid encases it all. I even have a client whose light bubbles change, depending on where he is— purple if he's in a crowded mall and pink if he's at a family gathering.

My client Elizabeth had crippling and debilitating social anxiety. Every time she attempted to go to the grocery store, she wouldn't make it halfway through an aisle without becoming extremely overwhelmed and then abruptly leaving. This anxiety had been plaguing her for more than 15 years. I taught her how to protect herself using the method you just learned. So after setting an intention, she'd put on her super shield, which consisted of two big, razor-sharp, white blades that spun around her wherever she went, in the shape of a cylinder. Elizabeth imagined that the blades were piercing, and as they spun, sliced away everything that wasn't of the highest good and about to serve her in a positive way. By using her shield when she went into public places where she felt bombarded with anxiety and other people's energy, Elizabeth could finally function. She felt safe and clearheaded; she was ready to confidently pursue the rest of her detox from a calm space.

Go with the Flow

During the first half of this program, especially your first three days, you may experience emotional, energetic, and/or physical "side effects." Although you're only in the initial protection stage of this program, having the intention to learn about and raise your vibration plugs you into a bigger, universal energy that affects your mind and body. Students have told me that they feel tired, get headaches, suffer from IBS or nausea, cry, scream, vomit, feel breathless and dehydrated, and deal with stomach aches as early as a week *before* their class or detox begins! This happens because energy and emotions are attached to body parts and organs, and your highest self knows you're about to release and cleanse some serious energy. This is a good thing; your energy gets a head start, so to speak. Clients also tell me they have the best sleep of their life or feel boundless energy both before and during a detox. There's always a handful of clients who wake up around 4 A.M. and feel drawn to walk the labyrinth at our retreat center, since they feel so revitalized. So be prepared: your body may feel new feelings that demand your attention. Follow their lead; this may be energy moving through you.

Grounding is a good complement to energetic work. The crown chakra is usually activated whenever energy work is involved, so it needs to be balanced with the root chakra, which can ground and stabilize all the energy that's traveling through the crown, to prevent short circuit side effects. Anytime you need to ground yourself, try this simple breathing exercise that centers and connects you to your energy. Find a quiet place to sit or lie down for five to ten minutes (or for as long as you need to feel relaxed). Next, breathe in for three counts, hold for three counts, and then exhale for three counts. Do several repetitions of this breathing pattern, and don't feel rushed. Sink into the clearing and relaxation it creates. If you'd like to go deeper, you can try the breaths with five counts each time. For an even more advanced grounding, inhale and imagine receiving positive, rejuvenating, and healing energy from the sky, in the color of your choice. Hold this breath for three counts and imagine it expanding throughout your body and into your cells. When you exhale, imagine releasing all the negativity you've absorbed throughout the day. PS: All of these grounding exercises are useful anytime you want to feel calm or centered—waiting in a long line, taking a relaxing walk during your lunch break, driving to the doctor, and so on.

MY FIRST SHIELD

Learning to create a protective shield changed my life. Before I mastered this, I was in a constant state of fear, anxiety, or, overwhelm, and other low vibrational feelings. Intense external energy darted at me from conversations oozing with stress or depression, highway road rage, or annoying text chains that made me want to punch a hole in the wall. I felt *so* out of control. At work, I was quick to snap, and everything felt like a level 10 catastrophe. I had trouble managing and establishing boundaries with employees and paying our company's bills on time. I felt caught in a rat race one day and stuck in place the next as if my feet were glued to the ground. I couldn't see the great work my company was producing, much less feel proud of its achievements. Weirdest of all? I realized that if a colleague sent me a perfectly neutral e-mail while they were in a bad mood, I could *feel* that person's heavy, chaotic energy! This was all before I learned to clear energy.

Going to the airport was the worst. The crowded space, rushing past other travelers who were trying to figure out flight details and get to the gate on time, the anger I'd feel if my own flight was delayed or canceled, the business calls I'd make while waiting for takeoff that never seemed to go right. All of these events put me in a frazzled and punchy state, every time.

When my psychic friend Christel and healer Nick explained that the discomfort I felt was being caused by external energy glomming onto mine, I was incredibly relieved. They were the first to teach me how to create protection—and *almost immediately*, the energy in and around me changed. Initially, I used an effective but rudimentary technique of surrounding myself with a white light bubble of protection, which worked perfectly fine. But I had an intuitive sense that I could do more for myself and for others when it came to creating protection from outside forces.

As I gathered and created the energy shielding techniques that I just taught you, protection gave me *freedom*, and it will do the same for you. You can go anywhere, do anything, and be with anyone you choose—with no toxic consequences. Designing protection that lets you exist in your own, clear energy allows the world to be your oyster. And when you detox your energy even more and routinely live on an elevated vibe? You won't need protection at all.

BUILDING A SHIELD CUES UNIVERSAL ACTION

During this initial phase of your purge, you will likely notice a subtle, energetic shift in the world around you. As I noted earlier, important synchronicities will ask you to pay attention to how your energy now interacts with others' and how the universe operates in general. Emotional issues that you've swept under the rug will sneak back out so you can resolve them, and problems you've tried to ignore because you couldn't handle them will feel prescient. Acknowledge and handle these cues and nudges as best you can, but don't let them frustrate you. Once you clear and elevate your energy, you'll be able to deal with them for good.

Recent energy shifts don't only bring troubling news—you'll also experience inspiring, positive shifts. Heartwarming dreams, new opportunities, and purposeful relationships will beam into your life too. All detoxes, energy or otherwise, clear the past. Out with the old, in with the new! So when you shield yourself from external energy, you protect yourself from what doesn't serve you and leave space to deal with what does. Rest assured that all this shifting and reshaping indicates that the universe is reshuffling its plans for you, and when you're finally in alignment by the end of the detox, you'll be well equipped to make changes from a purified state.

All humans are guided by a higher power that longs to put you on a spiritual path, but it's hard to sense this until you signal to the universe that you're ready to clear energy—and this starts with building a protective shield. The moment you do, it feels like your eyes pop open to God's signs and how the universe drops breadcrumbs for you to follow that keep you safe and moving toward your goals. Signs have always existed, but earthly distractions and energy blocks make them hard to see. But now, you'll notice divine signs everywhere! Plus, the more you acknowledge them, the more the universe will send. Staying open to receiving signs, remaining aware that they're coming, and feeling the intention to follow them is a potent and conscious combination that puts you on a vibration to invite the most exciting signs out there. When you create a shield, you're inevitably telling God that you're all in, and you set a path in motion to clear negative energy and devote yourself to using your gifts and pursuing your purpose work.

By making a shield, you also signal to the universe that you *believe* in its trusted guidance. Belief equals faith, which makes your detox even more effective, your energy clear faster, and your gifts activate more quickly. The energy and purity behind belief is like fuel to an engine; it not only starts the motor but determines how fast and effectively it runs. Believing that we're all created by God to have balanced energy and pursue our purpose work while using our gifts, is how we're innately wired. To be clear, these are all spiritual beliefs, which are different than religious ones. Religion involves a set of organized beliefs and practices, whereas spirituality is about individual practices that focus on finding peace and purpose. I've taught clients who hold tight to their Christian, Jewish, Muslim, and even atheist beliefs—and still benefit from energy detoxes. That's because energy is who you are; it's in your core. It isn't related to religion. No matter what your faith is, and how devotedly you practice it, you can be a gifted soul who's sensitive to energy. I'll never forget an atheist client who, while detoxing, had visions of Jesus and tall, glowing angels. The whole scene freaked him out but also expanded his belief that the universe is full of more souls, and operates so differently, than he thought. The tentpoles of what I teach about energy apply to every faith, culture, and background.

PROTECTION + VIBRATION

Protecting your energy helps you to begin raising your vibration, since you're no longer influenced by outside negativity that could lower it. If you're cruising along on a high vibration when your dad calls to criticize you for not making enough money, you won't drop to a lower level because your shield will preserve your energy. Though you'll learn how to fully clear your energy in the next chapter, protecting yourself from outside energy now and in the future helps keep you in your most natural state— which is not a low one. In fact, when you're in your most pure state, it mirrors the one you were born with and enjoyed during early childhood. You feel vibrant, fun, and creative. It's who you were before traumas and social setbacks knocked you down. What did you naturally love to do as a child? Were you helpful or kind? Chatty with strangers? Shy and book smart? According to my mom I was, apparently, a playful, inquisitive, bold, and silly kid. I loved playing soccer, hanging out with my cousins, making music, and clomping around in nature. It's fun to see these traits reflected in my sons too; when I need to reconnect with my authentic self, I kick around a ball or go for hikes with my kids. My client Natalie told me that when she wants to raise her vibration, she runs her hand over the tops of wildflowers like she did as a child. It engages so many senses and helps clear energy and reconnect with her inner child.

In the next chapter, I'll teach you how to clear your energy so it's in its purest state for when you learn how to raise its frequency. This is when like-minded and like-vibrational people and situations will begin to find you— and all others will fall away. Your detox is on a roll!

More Resources and Free Downloads

I've put together a powerful "Energy Shielding and Protection" meditation that you can listen to every morning that will prevent you from absorbing negative energy throughout the day. Download it for free at www.SpiritualActivator .com/protection

---

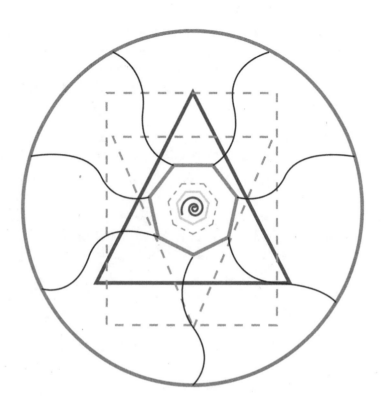

Chapter 4

DAYS 4-6: CLEAR YOUR ENERGY

IT'S TIME TO CLEAR some energy! Now that you feel safe inside your protection of choice, we're going to get rid of all the funk that's lodged inside that bubble. This negative energy comes from your environment, as well as the vibrations that pour from your own thoughts and emotions. They might surface when you're triggered by other people or situations, but it's the subsequent internal processing that leads to problematic self-talk, disappointments, shame, grief, and other dark emotions. This creates heavy energy that attaches to you like magnets to a refrigerator. But with your will and dedication, you'll pry them loose and finally feel free of the terrible emotional, spiritual, and often physical problems that have weighed you down for so long.

As I mentioned in Chapter 2, the most harmful energetic blocks come from the environment, internal traumas, and familial sources like generational and gestational memories that leave you feeling drained and defeated. They can also come from karmic issues that get lodged in your energetic body based on choices made during prior lifetimes. And if you're really sensitive to energy, you can even become energetically contaminated from someone thinking about you in other states or countries! The longer you go without detoxing this mucked-up energy, the more firmly it becomes fixed in your energetic body. See why clearing is necessary?

In the prior chapter, you took measures to protect yourself from new sources of energy so they don't attach to you or your auric field throughout the day. But that doesn't help the energy *already lodged* inside your energetic self, particularly your auric field and chakras. Remember, your auric field is the energetic skin that surrounds your body; it's what you use to sense other people's energy and what's happening around you. And then there are your chakras, which are the energy centers in your body that correspond to specific nerve bundles and major organs. They run along your spine from the crown of your head to the base of your spine. Your chakras need to stay open, or unblocked, to function well—and so you don't experience emotional, spiritual, or physical symptoms related to their qualities. Most energy healers focus on clearing their seven main chakras, but I've added an eighth. We'll go over them later in the chapter.

For the next three days, you will focus on clearing your auric field and chakras so that your soul can return to its highest and most empowered state—its natural way of being. Once you start to clear this energy, you'll feel free enough to use your purified vibration to step into spiritual gifts and purpose work. And, you don't have to remove every last bit of negative energy to feel significantly better. Clearing the root of blocks from your field and chakras is often enough to heal traumatic, environmental, and familial issues. That's the fun of detoxing—you never know how it will affect you! It's like going on a liver cleanse to aid digestion, and then losing 10 pounds and healing your eczema as a bonus.

Auric field and chakra clearing is the foundation for all healing. When I first learned to clear energy, I channeled that you must clear the auric field and chakras at the same time to produce the best results. It's like with weight loss: you can lose more weight, faster, when you combine clean eating with exercise, versus choosing one over the other. And similar to your three days devoted to creating protection shields, figuring out which clearing techniques work for you is also a personal and intuitive process. Especially when it comes to conducting impromptu clearings, you'll want to play with a few different practices to land on the best ones.

In this chapter, I'll explain where internal toxins come from, what to expect from a clearing and when to do them, how to clear your field and chakras, and how happiness and calm lend themselves to healing. Though it may sound like a big job to remove years of dense energy, this process doesn't have to be stressful. You're about to remove horrible stagnancy through the power of intention, visualization, and channeled energy from the universe to help you coast through life with a smile. You'll be bowled over when you finally experience life as the happiest version of you.

WHEN TO DO YOUR CLEARINGS

Clearings should happen first thing in the morning and at night, either when you come home from a busy day or at a quiet time before bed. You can also do impromptu clearings throughout the day to remove intense energy as needed. In the morning, you'll start by re-creating your protection shield. By now, re-creating your shield every morning is part of your daily routine, since you take it everywhere you go. When you're ready, you will then clear your auric field and chakras. There are three steps to clearing, and I suggest learning all of them on Day 4, and using Days 5 and 6 to get them down pat.

To recap, Days 1–6 of your detox help you protect yourself and understand what makes your energy vulnerable to toxins—and during Days 4–6 of energy clearing, you'll intuitively try out various techniques to figure out what works for you. Though I've allotted three days for clearing, you're welcome to extend it for up to an additional three days if you need to clear more deeply or simply rest. When you clear energy, the goal is to invite authentic energy into your energetic body, and eventually be able to discern what energy is yours and what belongs to someone else. You'll be surprised at how much energy you unknowingly pick up from others!

After a clearing, clients report that their overall feelings often change from, say, unsettled, anxious, and uncertain to confident, peaceful, and relaxed. Others experience fortuitous events like a promotion at work, a better relationship with an ex, sweet memories with their children, or a windfall of unexpected cash. You might also experience divinely sent coincidences that you desperately crave or need to survive. For instance, after my client Kara's labs showed high levels of thallium in her blood on Day 4 of the cleanse, she was extremely worried—that is, until a day later, when she happened to read in a magazine that eating a lot of kale, which she'd been doing, could cause a hyper-accumulation of this heavy metal in the blood! When Kara changed her diet, her levels normalized. Another example is how, on Day 6 of my student Marie's cleanse, she saw her chiropractor for an adjustment despite being low on money after paying down her college loans. Her chiro was so sympathetic to Marie's situation that he generously offered to treat her pro bono. Finally, you can do an impromptu clearing after a situation emotionally triggers you. Did lunch with your sister make you irritable or a disagreement with your co-worker leave you downright pissed? If so, clear this energy after your encounter. When I began clearing energy, I always picked up vibes from others that made me feel antsy. So I'd clear my shoes after walking through a crowded food court, clear the dentist chair before climbing in, clear a seat at the movie theater—endless clearings, all day long. But fear fueled my clearing practices, and I realized that I was attracting negative scenarios that made me need to clear in the first place! When I became aware of this, I limited my impromptu clearings to three a day. I think you'll find that's sufficient for you too.

Energy Release During Sleep

One of the reasons that you need to clear in the morning isn't just that it's a great way to start your day; it's also easy to energetically wake up on the wrong side of the bed. Think about it: How often do you feel a little glum or out of sorts when you first open your bleary eyes? That's because tons of energetic activity, transferring, and clearing happens when you sleep, and mattresses can hold on to that energy. And if you share your bed with another person, even a pet, they energetically process and clear their feelings while sleeping—and you can absorb this energy while processing and dumping yours at the same time. Just think of how often you stew and fret before bed or in the middle of the night, when you can't sleep. Or how you feel while watching the news or answering annoying e-mails in bed. If you have negative or fearful thoughts or feelings about work, family, your ex, reality TV characters, or a tragic war in another country, all of these thoughts and feelings create energetic ties that cling to you and your bed. And don't forget about the energetic heft of your and your bedfellow's dreams! Any time my empathic wife hangs out with her cousin, who produces true crime shows for a living, I know Mandy and I are in for an energetically fraught sleep. After seeing her cousin, Mandy dreams about the gory murders her cousin's show investigates, even if they don't talk about them. Guess who picks up on that shocked, terrified, and anxious energy? You got it. *I do.*

HOW TO CLEAR TOXIC ENERGY

The best way for you to clear your energetic body is from the outside in, mostly because it's efficient and easy to remember. Think of it like cleaning a car—first, you wash the exterior, and then you detail the interior. This means you'll begin by clearing the auric field around your body, which is where so many blocks live, and then move to the blocks that are stuck in your chakras. Finally, I'll teach you how to ground yourself after clearing both centers. Remember that during all of this, you will remain encased in your protection as you visualize and clear your energetic body. The more layers of protection and healing you can apply, the more powerful the cleanse.

STEP #1: CLEAR YOUR AURIC FIELD

First, set an intention to release all the energetic blocks and cords attached to you and your will. Something like, "God, please help me release all of these blocks and energetic cords that are draining me of my energy and vitality. Guide me as I clear these for the highest good of all."

Next, imagine yourself in the middle of a vortex, a giant swirl or tornado that's calmly but quickly whirling around you. Vortexes are powerful forces of energy that connect you to your spirituality. They're transformational energy centers where metaphysical energy can enter the earth or project out of the earth's surface. Sometimes I imagine myself creating the vortex around my body; I use my right hand to create a circular motion that builds around me until I can feel its energy. In the middle of this spinning funnel, state the intention, "Anything that's to be released from me will either go up to the sky or down to Mother Earth to neutralize." Or "All cords are removed and released, across all dimensions, times, and planes, never to return again."

The next step is to cut energetic cords in your field; this will slice the connections that you share with people or situations who've caused you distress in any way. To do this, you can imagine cords as glowing umbilical cords, energetic tubes flowing between you and others, or even a tree branch that attaches you to a person or place. I don't see cords, but many psychics do. Cords can transmit energy, information, body pains, and emotions between you and other people, which increases your intuitive pull and connection to them. When they're good, they can be very helpful; but when they're draining, they must go. Cutting cords is a main form of auric field clearing because this dominant form of energy, if it isn't eradicated, will feed directly into your chakras. This can progress into more serious conditions.

Slashing energetic cords that connect you to hurtful people and memories not only clears these negative influences but also lets you exist in only your own, clear energy going forward. While still in your vortex, start by filling yourself up with a color like purple, gold, or white, and then imagine your dominant hand as a pointy, sharp sword. Imagine the energy building behind and around this sword, and when it's at its max, move your arm in a cutting or swiping motion to slice the cords above, in front of, behind, and underneath you. You don't need to visualize all the people and places connected to these cords, but if specific ones come to mind, you can certainly imagine them disconnecting from you at this time.

If you don't like the idea of cutting or slicing (perhaps it feels too aggressive or violent), you can pull cords from various bodies or situations as if unplugging an electrical cord from a wall or pulling weeds from a garden. Then with a sweeping motion using both hands, imagine your hands as brooms or gathering a pile of weeds or cords lying on the ground, and throw them into the earth or sky for the universe to purify. Finally, you don't want to leave empty voids in your field or chakras that can potentially fill with negative energy. Set the intention to infuse these holes with love and imagine a color that resonates with you and makes you feel safe or at peace in order to plug the holes. A strong intention statement is, "I'm filling these holes with purple, and purple is divine love." The meaning of a particular color may change from person to person. To me, purple represents divine love but for someone else it may represent healing.

And just like that, your auric field is clear.

The Role of Imagination

Imagination plays an essential role in most spiritual practices. It's used in visualization, meditation, dreaming, manifestation—and for our purposes, clearing and healing your energetic body. Imagination, mixed with intention, colors, and sacred geometry, creates and accesses beneficial energy. It turns deeply held fantasies into reality, very quickly.

All ideas begin in the mind before becoming reality. In a similar, spiritual sense, your imagination creates thoughts and ideas in your brain, which carry high vibrational energy that taps into a supernatural reality and opens spiritual doors. Once you initiate this process, you begin to see signs from the universe, and serendipitous opportunities begin to fall at your feet. When your mind receives feedback, or proof, that convinces it that you've created these events, the powerful frequency of belief is initiated. Confidence in your beliefs, coupled with faith in a higher power, frees your mind to accept that imagination isn't a silly process that produces the occasional fluke. It's the prerequisite for a high vibrational life and miracles at every turn.

Your imagination is a robust, energetic bridge that links your 3-D brain and body to a divine space. I've channeled, too, that exercising your imagination strengthens this bridge—plus, the natural flow of love and connection between you, God, and the co-creation process during practices like prayer, setting intentions, manifesting, and energy clearing. Spending time in an imaginative space while making art, taking photos, creating music, dancing, or playing games with a child will bolster your imagination and thus all angles of your intuitive abilities too.

STEP #2: CLEAR YOUR CHAKRAS

Clearing chakras is a very mystical, energetic process. It leans on intuition, imagination, and a studied knowledge of what each chakra means to your spiritual, emotional, and physical bodies. The more connected you feel to each chakra and the body parts they impact, the more aware you'll become when your chakras speak to you in a way that you can't ignore. I've included a chakra chart at the end of this section so that you can learn what each chakra means and how to recognize, other than through a body scan, when they're blocked. There is a lot of information online about the origin and meaning of chakras too, if you'd like to dive further into this topic.

To start the chakra clearing, rub your hands together to create friction and activate the heat energy in your hands. Then, move your hands along your body, about an inch away from your skin, starting at your crown chakra and finishing at your root chakra. This is how you will scan for blocked energy. Your hands may feel intense heat or a magnetic pull when you find a messy chakra that demands clearing. This upset energy center might make you feel nauseous, tingle, or make your ears ring. My client Kristine's hands rhythmically pulse when she hits upon a chakra that needs clearing. The scanning process is different for everyone, but you will notice a difference in either your dominant scanning hand or your body as you do it. Your intuition and divine guidance will make sure you don't miss out on the chance to clear toxic energy!

When you encounter a blocked chakra, there are many ways to remove the energy—so again, you may want to play with a few practices until you find one that feels right to you. When I clear a chakra, I like to envision my hand as a sword and then cut out all the gunk that's inside my chakras. Once I'm finished, I cup my dominant hand, like a garden hand shovel or a scoop used in the bulk foods aisle of a market, and simply scoop the negative energy out of the chakra and then throw it into the ground or sky. You can also imagine toxins as tree branches that need to be trimmed or weeds that need to be pulled by their roots—and then tossed into the sky or ground. I've also had clients extract what they say feels like a sticky goo from chakras, and others pull the negative energy out as if it were a rope. You may have just one blocked chakra, or many—and some may require longer clearings than others, depending on how messy they are. Regardless, you'll know when you're finished because your body will feel lighter, and you'll instinctually know there's nothing left to extract. Finally, set an intention like, "God, please fill my cleansed chakras with your divine healing and love," and then fill the empty, cleansed chakras with divine, colored light from the sky (you can't go wrong with white, purple, or gold).

As a final step, a lot of healers make sure all chakras are spinning, but that's not necessary. Chakras are smart and divinely guided. In the same way that you don't need to tell the heart to beat, you don't need to tell chakras to rotate. They do this automatically. What's more important is that they're all the same size. When chakras are different proportions, they cause energetic imbalances. For example, if your crown is too big and root is too small after meditating, you might feel floaty and forgetful; you can miss commitments, drive past your exit on the highway, or forget half the items on your to-do list. Or if you get into a fight with a colleague, your solar plexus chakra, the center of your personal power, could become outsized compared to your heart chakra, which lacks empathy during an argument. To avoid these kinds of mishaps, imagine molding each chakra to the size of a tennis ball, similar to how you'd form a snowball with one hand. Ta-da! Your chakras are clear and balanced.

Get to Know Your Chakras

I think of chakras as swirling balls of energy that represent where the physical and conscious meet. They are ancient and powerful, and gurus have been working with these energy centers for thousands of years. Chakras align with the spine, and many diagrams show them stacked on top of one another, like spaced out vertebrae throughout the human system. There are seven major chakras, but during a channel, I was shown an eighth one—the ear. Here they are:

Crown Chakra: Located in the top center of your skull. This is where your physical body and consciousness meet your higher self and the collective consciousness. The crown chakra helps you spiritually grow and raise the vibration of humanity, plus connect with divine knowing. Society's and the material world's needs will heavily affect this chakra. Its message is about letting go of the physical, singular consciousness to become one with the collective.

When it's blocked: Blocks here can be very serious. Those who are extremely materialistic and have a hard time letting go will often have a block in the crown. It may even create disconnection between the mind and body, plus your ability to feel empathy. When your crown chakra is unblocked, you can easily receive messages and guidance from your higher power.

Third-Eye Chakra: Located in the middle of your forehead, in the space between your eyes. Your third eye correlates with intuition, a place of spiritual and psychic knowing. An open and balanced third eye means you're in tune with the spiritual and energetic world around you, and you're able to access the positive sides of most situations. Your ability to think and make decisions, plus imagination and memory, affect this chakra. You can tap into the past, present, and future using your third eye. For some, it can help you to astral travel, where your consciousness separates from your physical body and travels throughout the astral plane. You can also use it to practice remote viewing, which is when a person can give information about an object, event, person, or location that's hidden from view and at a physical distance. What's more, a balanced third eye allows you to communicate with spirits on the other side if this is your gift, while others might use it to see a person's energy and auric field. It also guides your intuition and that sense of "knowing" that so many spiritually adept people have.

When it's blocked: This can get blocked due to issues with the lower chakras. In fact, if one of the first five chakras is out of balance, it is highly likely that the third eye is too. If you have difficulty with intuition or feel judgmental or dismissive of others, your third eye is probably blocked. Physically, this block can present with headaches, dizzy spells, and brain health.

Ear Chakra: Located in the ears, the right ear symbolizes male influences that are connected to the cause of the block, and the left, female influences that do the same. Your ear chakras are vulnerable to words you've heard; angry, gossipy, toxic vibrations can be carried by the sound of a person's voice and get absorbed through the ear chakra. If your ear chakras are sensitive, you might love music, books read aloud, and be an auditory learner.

When it's blocked: Your self-esteem dips, and you engage in negative self-talk. You become sensitive to sounds and hate loud noises. Criticism sticks to you like glue.

Throat Chakra: Located at the center of the throat, this chakra is about communication. It's related to speaking your authentic truth, plus listening to others and your deepest self. It demands that you pay attention to your wants, needs, and wishes. If you're communicating with those who aren't listening, this will greatly affect this chakra's balance. It can also be thrown off when you refuse to listen to your higher self and consciousness.

When it's blocked: The throat chakra becomes blocked when you hold in your emotions and beliefs versus saying them aloud. A fear of expressing yourself could be related to trauma, difficulty putting your feelings into thoughts and words, or a shy spirit. You might fear judgment from others. Physically, you can develop a sore throat or thyroid problems from this block.

Heart Chakra: Sits near your heart, in the center of your chest. This chakra is all about love and spiritual awareness. It's one of my favorite chakras to work with. A balanced heart chakra will lead to inner peace and allow love and compassion to flow freely from, and to, you.

When it's blocked: A block here can be very serious. It can lead to feelings of anger, betrayal, jealousy, and resentment. These feelings create serious mental issues like depression and anxiety. It can physically show up as medical problems with the heart, circulation, and lungs. You also tend to attract toxic people into your life who drain your energy. You might find it difficult to receive thoughtful presents, acts of kindness, or compliments from others.

Solar Plexus Chakra: This chakra is located above the belly button, at the base of the chest. It represents personal power and controlling your self-esteem. Feeling confident and in control is related to this chakra. It affects your fears, anxiety, and feelings of purpose. Physically, it affects metabolism and the digestive system. Gut health and eating well are essential to its balance.

When it's blocked: Blocks here can have serious and damaging effects on spiritual, physical, and mental states. If you're blocked here, you are often indecisive and have anger and control issues. You may also have a hard time standing in your power around others and controlling your emotions. You can swing from happy to sad in a split second, unable to find balance or inner peace. A blocked solar plexus chakra also affects how connected you feel to others, whether you're having and enjoying new experiences and setting healthy boundaries. Physical manifestations show up in the digestive system, such as diabetes or hypoglycemia.

Sacral Chakra: Found just below the belly button, at the base of the stomach. The sacral chakra relates to sexual and creative energies. When it's balanced, you'll naturally experience self-love and have an equally harmonious and nurturing relationship with the people and environment around you. You'll express yourself with skill and instinctually know to set healthy boundaries.

When it's blocked: You have a hard time going after what you desire in life. You may fear change or have "addictive behaviors" toward food, alcohol, sugar, even people. A blocked sacral chakra can cause reproductive issues and affect your intimacy and sexual expression with others.

Root Chakra: Located at the base of the spine, where it meets the pelvis. This relates to how grounded you are, your survival instincts, and your basic needs—physical and mental. The root chakra correlates to how secure you feel too. Your food and water intake, the space you call home, and finances contribute to its balance. Releasing fear can lead to a clear root chakra.

When it's blocked: Physical issues arising from a blocked root chakra include pain or problems in the colon, lower back, bladder, legs, and feet—basically the lower areas of your body. Emotional or

spiritual issues include anxiety, fear, body disasso-
ciation, and poor boundaries. This blocked chakra
can also lead to financial issues and an inability to
"make things happen."

STEP #3: GROUND YOURSELF

After clearing your auric field and chakras, it's essential to ground yourself. Clearing energy and dismantling blocks can use a lot of crown and third-eye chakra energy, so even if you've rebalanced them, it's possible that you still feel the "floaty" aftereffects of a clearing.

I'd like you to first stand with your feet slightly apart and imagine them fixed to the ground like roots from a tree extending a foot into the mud beneath you. Breathe in through those roots, up into your feet, then your body, and out your head or crown and into the sky above.

Next, I want you to raid the kitchen for salty and earthy food. Salt clears energy. You can put a little salt under your tongue or sprinkle it on top of your feet or in your hands. Or you can eat a few salty crackers or food grown in the ground and connected with earth energy like potatoes or rice. Strategic nourishment goes a long way when you feel drained and heady after a clearing. You might also find that you're craving sugar or alcohol, which numbs out energy and takes the edge off your intuition so that you're not as sensitive or connected to what's around you. I believe this is why, in my experience, detectives stereotypically meet at a bar for drinks while handling a hard case or why some mediums crave sugar after a reading; subconsciously, they want to turn off their energy, and booze and sugar are surefire ways to do it. My client Gena, a natural empath, craved steak and burgers while going through a breakup, because this food was so grounding for her. Energetically, it made her root chakra big so that she could stand up to her ex, but her third eye shrank because her arguments didn't include intuitive empathy for what he was feeling. After she ended the relationship, she was careful to clear her energy and rebalance her chakras' sizes. She also went on a vegan diet for two weeks to clear the physical effects of all that red meat!

IMPROMPTU ENERGY CLEARINGS

As I mentioned earlier, there may be times that you feel the need to clear energy after being in a tense situation that you can feel affecting you. By the end of Day 6, I'd like you to have practiced the following quick and simple impromptu exercises, and then choose a few to keep in your back pocket for when you need to clear energy in a pinch. My client Faith, who I met in one of my workshops, worked in a car dealership. By Day 5 of her detox, Faith found it difficult to deal with so many of her clients' haphazard energies all day. She often needed to move her body to clear her energy, but because of her schedule, she didn't have time to go for a run or hit the gym when she felt pent up. I suggested Faith shift her energy by shutting her office door, putting on headphones, and dancing for 10 minutes. To change things up, Faith added in jumping jacks and push-ups. Sure enough, her energy cleared every time—and returning to work was a cinch.

Note: These techniques in isolation, without protecting or cleansing yourself in the way I've just taught you, are *not enough* to clear all the energy in your field and chakras. They're situational hacks if you know you're having lunch with an argumentative friend or hopping on a call with a frustrated family member. After, you can do a quick clearing to kill off consequent toxins. Think of these as easy cleaning solutions, like using hand sanitizer. Done and done.

- Physical movement like exercise, swimming, jogging, dancing, and yoga
- Enjoying nature: taking deep breaths in the sun or walking barefoot in the grass or on the beach
- Taking long drives
- Using a citrine crystal near or on your body (sometimes these are sold as necklaces) or a selenite wand to clear negative energy. You can also put the wand in the corner of a room or in your bed to keep these spaces free of bad vibes. You'll learn more about crystals in Chapter 5.
- Burning incense, sage, and palo santo. I'm a fan of palo santo because it doesn't have as strong a fragrance as sage. Most sage has antimicrobial properties, and some is antibacterial, so when you clear energy with it, you're also clearing the energy of bacteria, fungi, and viruses. When I burn sage, I run it over my entire body while saying, "Clear, clear, clear."
- Taking an hour to read a book, journal, or meditate. Alone, you're with only your energy and automatically connected on an unconscious level to a higher power who clears energy.
- Geometric breathing. In two cycles, breathe in for five counts and imagine all the negativity that's collected in your heart as a dense fog or

liquid. Hold that breath for five counts, and then exhale all the excess energy that you don't want. And since whatever you remove needs to be replaced, imagine filling yourself back up with love or a color or image that represents love to you. When you follow the cycle of this technique, it builds a sacred geometry for clearing.

- If someone specific is upsetting you, send them off in a "love bubble." Set the intention to send love to this person, imagine a color coming down from the sky that exemplifies love (pink, purple, and gold are popular), and wrap that person in this colored bubble and send them into the heavens until you don't see the person or bubble anymore. At this point, their energetic cords detach from yours and remove their influence on you. This is great after an upsetting text chain.

FEELINGS, THOUGHTS, AND BEHAVIORAL ENERGY

Going forward, remember that disempowering internal energy originates with thoughts, feelings, choices, and the act of processing situations in your past and present. All of this creates an energetic output, and the more negative it is, the more you contribute to a block. The progression of thought > emotion > behavior or decision carries an extremely powerful frequency. The more you focus on this pattern, the louder and more solidified it becomes. So bad things can happen to you all day long, *but how you respond to them* is what fuels and feeds a damaging block.

If you don't cleanse and shift your energy after responding in an unsavory way, you'll stay on a low frequency where all kinds of discouraging things will find you: new bills, car problems, work troubles, spats at home, tech issues. This becomes your reality! You also absorb negative energy from Debbie Downers on your same vibration, and their energy becomes lodged in your auric field and chakras too. Energy cords form between you and these buzzkills, and harmful energetic frequencies flow back and forth between you. Manifesting becomes impossible. You'll feel like a victim of bad fate or luck, but you are actually part of that life's creation—a self-fulfilling prophecy that'll increasingly pick up speed until you get ahead of it.

The techniques you've just used are very effective at removing all kinds of blocks, plus the thought, emotion, and behavioral energy that causes them. However, it takes six months of advanced training to learn how to master the healing of familial blocks, karmic work, and physical illnesses, so I won't specifically focus on those in this chapter or book. Even so, I've seen physical illnesses unexpectedly heal when clients clear their auric fields and chakras, if the illness's energetic root happens to be in these areas. Same goes for familial blocks. If you suspect your problems are related to familial blocks, you can set an intention before you clear like, "God, I'd like to release whatever familial blocks are holding me back and not for the highest good." You can always do the same for physical illnesses too: "God, I'd like to release any blocks related to my physical illness if it is for the highest good of all." Hey, it's worth a shot!

No matter what, a body riddled with low vibes and energy blocks has the capacity to go haywire since depressed and chaotic frequencies are not innate to the human body. *You were not born this way.* When you clear your field and chakras, you return to your truest self and experience your authentic energy—that which is unaffected by trauma, programming, outside influences, and blocks. It's the energy of a purified soul.

More Signs? You Bet

Once you clear the emotions, thoughts, and beliefs that have formed blocks in both your auric field and chakras, the universe will send you even more fun, helpful, and significant coincidences. They may be related to the blocks you're clearing, the spiritual path you're about to take, or simply validate that you're being guided. Common synchronicities include hearing songs relevant to the moment, seeing special numerical patterns (111 is a popular sign, said to symbolize new beginnings), and meaningful, timely animals crossing your path.

GO DEEP

Though it may take some time, getting to the root of a block is everything. The more you've fed toxic emotions, the more deeply they've become lodged in your energy field. Think about how your self-esteem could take a hit if you got laid off. Feeling less-than could graduate to feeling disposable, which becomes part of your personality. Now, you not only accept that you're expendable in your workplace, but in relationships and other areas. Your mind and energy system will adjust to this message and continue to fuel this energy even more. It then dictates a vibration that attracts disappointing friends and uninspired opportunities. You might think it's a fluke that you're suddenly spending time with subpar partners, your new job stinks, and you have lackluster friends, but what's really happening is that energy blocks are growing and solidifying. The original scenario that once annoyed you has now made you chronically sad, anxious, and lazy. Frustration, envy, guilt, shame, and feelings of inadequacy start to pile on as they plunge deeper into your field and chakras. Disease has the potential to form, and in time, all of this energy can settle into your cells and even your soul. You can see how clearing layers of energy makes a difference in your wellness—and if you hit upon the root of an issue, how it can dislodge multiple blocks at once and, frankly, change the entire scope of your world.

My client Brenda is a fascinating example of someone who cleared just one chakra—and because it was the root of her issues, saved her own life. When Brenda was a child, she developed a block in her heart chakra. It first began to grow when one day, she hugged her mother, who was an innately awkward and chilly woman. Mom reacted to Brenda's hug in an unexpected and uncomfortable way. She let out a little, "Oh!" then clumsily hugged Brenda back. Mom stammered, "I see! Okay! We're doing this now!"—and it left an upsetting impression on Brenda. And every time Brenda reached out for future hugs, her mom repeated this odd behavior. It didn't take long for Brenda to associate physical affection with the false belief that when it came to love, she must be uncomfortably imposing on others who didn't want to receive it. It wasn't an accident, then, that Brenda worked at a demoralizing job, married a narcissistic and verbally abusive man who took advantage of her vulnerability, and developed breast cancer in her thirties (many spiritual teachers believe that breast cancer is related to a blocked heart chakra). By the time Brenda found Mandy and me, her heart chakra was about to burst. I taught Brenda how to clear this jammed-up chakra, plus her auric field. Incredibly, just by clearing this one, albeit enormous, wound from her life, Brenda experienced a remarkable turnaround.

Within weeks, Brenda discovered her self-worth and made dramatic changes. All this time, she'd felt that her love was dangerous, but when she unblocked her energy, she viscerally understood otherwise. Brenda's life soared. She now had the booming confidence to find a new and more gratifying job, end her marriage, and reconcile with her mother. By mending her relationship with Mom, she began to heal other familial blocks. Best of all? Brenda's cancer went into remission. And to think such disorder began with a thought—the block's inception around which she built her life and belief system. All her thoughts, feelings, and behaviors fueled that reality—but no more. Brenda is a new woman who seeks real love and peace in all she does.

As with Brenda's story, I've noticed that the most overwhelming and debilitating block is usually the one that clears first. It doesn't matter that you have other blocks tucked inside your field or chakras. Your clearing will remove the most immediate need that's most relevant to your life at that time, and any blocks connected to it. Once that primary block is cleared, you can go back to work on deeper energetic toxins. Therefore, I've allotted three or more days for you to clear energy during this detox. Most of us intuitively know what our loudest problem is, so it may not be much of a surprise when you hit upon it. But it sure will be a relief when it's gone.

As you clear your aura and chakras, you may find that your body physically reacts to this process. Your heart may beat faster, or your stomach may be nauseated. This is because the energy targeting your chakras and auric field is being received by your physical body. In fact, sometimes the energy penetrates so deeply that it heals a physical ailment. After all, clearing blocks can change your emotional, spiritual, and physical state—as well as scenarios related to each of those blocks. Clearing the throat chakra could help you negotiate with an architect who's building your fantasy home and unblocking your sacral chakra could restore your sense of personal power when taking that first step toward turning a dream into a dream job. Once your blocks are cleared, your energy finds its natural flow. Just keep in mind that the extent to which your body clears isn't always up to you. You can identify and clear a block, but no matter how deep you go, it's ultimately up to God as to how much is lifted. There are blocks you'll be able to fix and others that will take a few weeks or even a month. So much of this could be related to the lessons you're meant to learn in this lifetime or heal in that moment for the highest good of all. Your vibration might even need to match the amount of healing your body can receive at that time. If prior to cleansing, you set the intention that "whatever is in the highest good to clear, will clear," then you will know you've done all you can to shift energy.

ALL TOGETHER NOW: *AAAAH*

Now that your energy is crystal clear, your body should feel light and your soul guided and intimately connected to your higher power. And if you were chronically depressed and anxious before your cleansing rituals, even a small emotional bump up to neutral is a monumental step forward. Make the most of this energy and mood shift! Grab coffee with a friend and quietly pay for a stranger's order. Go fishing with your kids and take them for ice cream after. Your intuition, throat, and heart are open for giving and receiving. Your ears are attuned to happy conversation, you're feeling creative, and your self-esteem is intact. You're feeling grounded, compassionate, and generous with your whole self. What an awesome improvement!

Next up, I'll teach you how to raise your vibration. It's essential to do this so that you can attract the people and opportunities that will match your brilliant, elevated state.

More Resources and Free Downloads

I've put together a powerful 15-minute meditation you can do daily before bed. This meditation quickly clears your chakras from all lower-level energies and frequencies you've encountered throughout the day. Download it for free at www.SpiritualActivator.com/clearyourenergy

---

Chapter 5

DAYS 7–9: ELEVATE YOUR ENERGY

MORE THAN HALFWAY THROUGH your detox, you now have simple morning, evening, and impromptu practices that seriously move the needle in your emotional, practical, and spiritual life. For one, I'll bet you're noticing a shift in your attitude and outlook, as you naturally lean in to optimism and peace. Your goals, wishes, and dreams are beginning to fall into place too. You feel increasingly connected to like-minded souls. And I'm downright certain that you're feeling amazed at the "coincidences" that are popping up to guide and validate your spiritual path.

The secret sauce, of course, is your protected and cleansed energetic body, which is vibrating higher than ever. Now it's time to learn how to raise that energetic bar *even higher*. Yes, you heard me right! You should be reaching for the stars when it comes to how high your vibration can go, go, go. After all, the more your frequency rises, the more you increase your ability to attract and co-create an incredible future with God and your higher self. I also find that raising your vibration is fun! I know a detox takes effort and practice to get the most out of it, but you must admit that watching your life transform is already a good time. And because enjoyment is such a pleasant, optimistic, and powerful emotional expression, having fun also carries a high frequency. So the more you play with vibration-raising techniques—even if they include relaxing all alone—the higher you'll go. This preps your energetic body to discover and then practice your spiritual gifts and purpose work in coming chapters.

Reaching for a high vibe is a lot like jumping on a trampoline—it's a safe and enjoyable way to bounce higher and higher. But ultimately, your end game is to make an elevated vibration *your way of life*. It's in this souped-up energetic body that incredible people and opportunities find you without effort. When I began living on an elevated frequency, problems started to solve themselves or simply avoid me. Anything I want now is within reach on this vibration, even things that I didn't know were possible. Issues that were once big became small, since I have more bandwidth to deal with them. Manifesting occurs shockingly fast, as my goals are fueled by a high frequency passion. It also feels natural to establish boundaries and speak my truth with family, friends, and colleagues who'd otherwise bring me down. At this point, you don't live in the same reality as everyone else; unhappy moments and instigating adversaries can't touch you.

Removing blocks that anchored you to a lower space was a huge step in clearing, purifying, and raising your vibration. Let's now use Days 7–9 to play with thoughts and techniques that will start your day on a super high vibration, rescue this frequency if it dips, and eventually sustain a stellar energy level so that you're rarely thrown off during a challenge—and if you are, help you recalibrate. What's always amazing to me is that when you eventually flow on a high vibration as a way of life, you won't even *need* to protect yourself or clear energy on a regular basis. Negative moments will roll off your back or just not affect you.

My client Jan is a perfect example of this. Her sister Lilly used to pick on her during her visits home for the holidays. Lilly would make digs about Jan's weight, her marriage, her parenting techniques, the size of Jan's home, and her income. But after detoxing, Jan raised her vibration so high, and was able to stay there, that Lilly's blows barely influenced her mood. It's no fun to poke at someone who doesn't fuel your fire, so Jan's sister backed off when she saw that her comments no longer got a rise out of Jan. Once Lilly simmered down and felt approachable, Jan told her that her judgments were hurtful and insisted that certain topics become off-limits when they spoke. Lilly didn't love that Jan was calling the shots this way, but she quickly realized that if she didn't fall in line with Jan's requests, she'd further risk her relationship with her sister as well as her nieces. It's been a year since Jan's tough conversation, and Jan and her sister are settling into a relationship that's comfortable for them both.

When Jan told me this story, I was so proud of her determination to establish realistic boundaries that helped her sustain a high vibration. The whole story brought a vivid image to mind. I pictured Jan's sister throwing rocks at her as Jan rode a bike on the sidewalk in front of her sister's house. Then I visualized her sister throwing rocks at Jan while she was in the sky on an airplane. Jan's sister could easily hit Jan with a few rocks and cause her to crash when the two were on similar planes. But when Jan's vibration soared high above the clouds, Lilly didn't have a chance at nailing her with a rock. Jan was flying high and well out of Lilly's reach.

Once your own vibration ascends, the simplest way to sustain it is with high frequency activities and environmental changes. In no time, these become part of your daily habits, like taking a shower or brushing your teeth. Frequency-raising activities are personal and different for everyone. They also raise your intuition, as you strengthen your third eye by choosing activities based on gut instinct. I love to take long drives to raise my energy, but you might like going for a run or doing photography. And since the people and opportunities in your midst gradually change to reflect your new vibration, you'll soon feel increasingly fortified by their fantastic energy too. You'll connect with those who mirror your values and inspire you to find happiness.

In this chapter, I'll suggest when to elevate your energy, activities to do the trick, how you'll feel when you're high, what to do when your vibe dips, and the two emotional states that enforce the strongest frequencies you can attain on earth. There's no stopping you now!

WHEN TO RAISE YOUR VIBRATION

As a daily practice, in addition to doing protection and clearing rituals in the morning and night, you will now add a vibration-raising exercise at both times. You can also use this as needed throughout the day, much like you do with impromptu clearings. So by the end of Day 9, I'd like you to discover and mentally log three to five outstanding, vibration-boosting exercises that lift your frequency. You'll find that eventually, you'll have a go-to exercise, plus a few backups in case you're in the mood for something different. That's the thing about energetic exercises—in the beginning, one exercise might be ideal, but over time and as you grow, you'll find that others may be better suited to your mood and lifestyle. It's also helpful to have a go-to exercise for everyday life, but when all hell breaks loose at the office or with the kids, you may want to stack or layer a few vibration-raising exercises to change the energy in and around you.

I like to layer activities to combat routines that have the potential to bring me down. For instance, I hate doing dishes, but I love to learn and laugh. So I listen to educational podcasts or a comedian's audiobook as I scrub plates and glasses to keep my vibration high during this bummer chore. Once I'm in a good mood, I like to journal about five events that made me feel grateful that day. Folding regular vibe-raising activities into your schedule reminds me of how, after a food cleanse, you choose which beneficial foods will best feed your body and lifestyle.

GETTING HIGH

Practices meant to raise your frequency should never feel forced or like work. If they do, you'll achieve the opposite of what you're going for: you'll drain your energy and depress your vibration. You want to feel instinctively drawn to your choices. They should make you smile, feel energized, and remind you that you're creating the best version of yourself en route.

Though we talked about clearing exercises in the last chapter, some energy-boosting activities clear *and* elevate at the same time. Though I don't want you to skip the clearing step, just know that if you encounter a vibration-lowering situation, you have the option to choose one of these clearing and energy-raising practices to knock out two goals at once. The easiest way to know that you've hit upon an activity that clears and raises is to follow the principle of natural wiring. This states that each of us comes to earth knowing instinctive ways to clear and elevate our energy. After all, our souls incarnate in a clear and high state, so returning to such purity is ideal and should feel natural. It's in this refined place that higher energy can flow through you, intended for the highest good. I briefly mentioned this in Chapter 3, when I talked about how your soul's best state mirrors the one you had as a child. Maybe you liked to walk barefoot in the grass, sing, or sit quietly by yourself and play with your toys. Your energy was at peace when you were doing these activities as a child, always clearing and raising, though you never knew it.

Returning to any practice, then, that reminds you of your inner child's mindset will transport you to the depths of your soul. In fact, the more evocative your activity—like keeping a poetry journal or fingerpainting as art therapy— the more effectively you'll raise your frequency. This is because emotional activities tap into energetic frequencies most profoundly. What's more, I've found that nature-related activities really resonate with natural wiring work. Some clients love to feel the sun or wind on their faces, while others like to be around fire or feel rejuvenated by water or digging in the soil or sand. I loved swimming in the ocean as a kid, so I like to take Epsom salt baths now. When you're exploring natural activities that lift you, hit spots that address multiple elements at once. At a local beach or pond, you can see how you feel as the sea breeze blows on your face, as well as what it's like to dig in the sand or build a sandcastle. After all, a variety of activities made your day as a child; you should expect the same as an adult.

This is to say, interests that speak to your most authentic self will have the most intense effect on your energy. All thoughts, emotions, and actions that rise from a soulful, sacred place multiply frequencies. Making music, art, movies, building, playing sound bowls, writing, and crocheting are popular options. Indulging in a massage and going for a thoughtful, long walk with a friend will also stir emotions that move stagnant, stale, and disempowering energy out of your body so higher energy flows through. Serving and doing acts of kindness can take your energy up a notch too. Holding a door for a stranger, sending a thank you card, and texting a gratitude note are all amplifying options. As you explore activities that boost your vibe, be sure to perform them with your best intentions in mind and for the highest good. Sharing, giving, caring, and moving through life with love and connection will bolster and steady your frequency. If you toss off a compliment to your sister or buy Starbucks for a homeless person without too much of an emotional investment, your energy won't budge since your open heart isn't in it.

If you feel more fulfilled when you're alone, detachment and isolation from others can just as easily recharge your energetic battery. My client Gemma attended one of my workshops feeling overwhelmed, anxious, and angry at the start. She'd driven 18 hours to see me, since she felt her entire life was falling apart and had nowhere else to turn. Though Gemma went through all my detox steps, by the time we got to vibration raising, she felt very jumpy and overwhelmed. Extreme energy tends to circulate during workshops, and it can be too much for very sensitive souls. This was the case for Gemma. Her psychic bandwidth was tapped.

Gemma began crying, rocking back and forth in the fetal position—and though she was too shy to tell me she wanted to leave, Gemma's body language screamed for escape. After our vibe-raising class ended, I looked out the window to see Gemma rolling her suitcase toward the parking lot. I was worried about Gemma and didn't know what to make of her sudden exit. I've never had a student leave a workshop without finishing! Cut to a few weeks later, when one of my top certified healers and workshop leaders named Fatou ran into Gemma at an airport—and thought Gemma looked amazing! Fatou said Gemma's energy now felt whole and at peace, and she believed that my detox workshop healed Gemma. Gemma said she felt like a new woman. I was so relieved to hear this and instinctually knew that what Gemma needed to raise her vibration wasn't a soul-searching group activity but solitude, her favorite tunes, and a long drive home through tree-shaded back roads. When she needed a boost, Gemma found it in solitude.

Another fascinating way to raise your vibration is with color energy therapy—it's a simple and powerful tool. Light is the fastest and strongest way to transmit a high frequency to your energetic body, right down to the cellular level. Light also travels faster than the speed of sound, so it transports energy quickly. Start by closing your eyes and setting an intention like, "I want to raise my vibration to a high and sustainable level." Next, imagine pure, healing light and energy running through your body. This light can be white, gold, purple—it doesn't matter, so long as the color symbolizes divinity to you. Imagine the light as focused and concentrated as you can, shooting down like a laser, so that it carries divine love within it. Picture this light streaming from the heavens, touching the top of your head, and then expanding to fill up your body. Make sure it reaches every corner of your being—from the top of your head to the tips of your toes. Now, let this light beam lift you into the sky—above your house, city, state, country, the world. Imagine following it as high as you can go. When you reach the heavens, you are as close to God as you can be. Bask in the light and love. Breathe it in for three seconds, hold for three seconds, and exhale for three more. Every part of you is now filled with the high vibrational energy you're breathing in. When you're ready, gently allow yourself to drift back to earth like a feather. On the ground, imagine roots growing from your feet and stretching into the earth. This will steady you, so that you don't feel floaty and balloon-headed all day.

As your energy raises, it will deliver an environment that serves the frequency you're now on. You'll find yourself indulging in passion projects with compatible personalities that make you feel safe, understood, and fully yourself. You'll no longer feel on guard or inadequate in others' company. You'll create a soul family that makes you feel accepted and celebrated, which causes your energy to soar even higher. Hosting a dinner for new friends won't feel like a social feat, but a casual meal. You'll feel at home in your body, mind, and the world around you.

Crystal Clear Vibrations

Crystals are a tremendous tool to help raise and sustain a high vibration. They can be a fascinating and compelling addition to your practices, but please know that you can raise your energy without them. I've seen students give away their power, thinking they can't move forward without a certain stone in hand, and that's not true. Whatever you can do with a crystal, you can do without one. When you use crystals, their purpose is meant to merely remind you of, or awaken, your innate abilities. Once you realize and internalize this, you can use crystals in a more advanced way while staying in your power. That said, I do have a few go-to stones that help me when I can use an assist or need to phone a friend.

I like to wear crystals around my neck or strategically place them in my room—on a nightstand, under the bed, or in a room's corners. Dark crystals like smoky quartz, obsidian, and black tourmaline protect against negative vibrations and block heavy energy coming from sources like spooky spirits and EMFs. Citrine is terrific for self-clearing, as it carries the energy of the sun; it dissolves low energy and replaces it with happy, rejuvenating vibes from a higher frequency. Selenite can activate and raise your vibration; they're also used during meditations, healings, and cleansing rituals. If you put a selenite wand in each corner of your room, they will call in the angelic realms and make it easier to interact with this dimension. Finally, I love amethyst for opening my crown chakra to sharpen visions and invite intuitive information and healing. Rose quartz opens anyone's heart, balancing emotional health and helping to release blocks. It's known to help the heart chakra heal from pain and trauma, bond you to friends and family, and remind you to always practice self-love and self-care too.

AN ALL-TIME HIGH

As you evolve from activities that raise your energy, bask in the feelings they evoke. Are you experiencing less fear and stress? Has the pit in your stomach disappeared? Are you grateful for the fact that so many positive emotions are your new normal? The future should feel exciting—which raises your energy even more and gives you good reason to celebrate growth.

The simplest way to evaluate the extent to which your vibration has changed is to compare how you feel now to how you felt prior to detoxing. You can also ask trustworthy confidants if they've noticed a difference. Now is also a great time to journal about how you've advanced since your detox began—and leave room to compare this time to how you feel a few months from now once you've sustained your groove. Consider: Are you anxious or sad? Do your friends still put you down, and if so, do you respond differently? Are you with the same partner, and if so, has that relationship changed? How's your energy level? Do you like or loathe your job? Do you feel like you've settled in life or are you fulfilled in most that you do?

As your vibration rises, and you feel drawn to restructure your world and the people in it, you may feel torn about spending time with old friends, colleagues, and family who bring you down and lower your frequency. We don't live in a perfect world where it's easy, or even a good idea, to shelter yourself from all low vibe triggers, so it's normal—and totally okay—for your energy to fluctuate as a result. You can't avoid all the effects that illness, grief, bad luck, trauma, or emotional friends have on you. And bolting from these feelings doesn't allow you to live a human experience, learn lessons, and grow your soul. Thriving on our earthy plane means adjusting to the complications that come with it and are out of your control. So when you face a tricky situation, don't freeze out Negative Nellies and run from hard talks. Respect others' past and pain, but use your clearing and raising tools. Respond with listening, love, and boundaries.

Creating boundaries with iffy personalities exercises your sacral and throat chakras, which empowers and heals. You might not speak your truth perfectly at first, and that's okay. Give yourself grace. Most of my clients overcorrect before establishing boundaries that are comfortable for everyone. Don't feel guilty or beat yourself up. Also, don't apologize for setting boundaries in the first place. The best way to stand in your truth is to start any boundary conversation with, "I love you, but/and . . ." This holds your energy intact, since you're putting love first. It will also help you channel divinely guided words for the highest good of all.

When my son Braydon was young, my father used to shame him if he didn't finish his meal or made a mistake on his homework. I wasn't too surprised when this first happened, since my dad was similarly critical of me while I was growing up. But for my son, my wife and I decided this was unacceptable. I had a strict talk with Dad and, in so many words, told him to cut it out—or else. My demanding tone was a bit over the top, which only caused my father to ignore me. So when I approached him a second time, I took a lighter yet still-firm hand. I said, "I love you, but you're not respecting the boundaries we established about Braydon's care, so we're going to distance ourselves until you learn how to respect boundaries." Note how I led this talk with love and didn't cut Dad off entirely; I also said that if he corrected his behavior, we'd happily let him spend more time with his grandson. This finessed discussion kept Dad in line and my energy high. Today, he has a warm relationship with both of my sons and decent respect for our limits.

WHEN YOUR VIBE IS IN TROUBLE

If I notice that my energy is dipping, and I don't correct my frequency immediately, the universe seriously lets me know. When I began healing and teaching, I set the intention, "God, if my frequency dips, please send me signs that are really obvious and in my face so that I can raise it again for the highest good of all." That way, when a vibe goes sideways, I can't miss the chaos around me. I'd like you to do the same so that the universe quickly cues you to self-correct. Though these signs might upset you at first, they're not bad news. They're a wake-up call from God, who's nudging you to work on your energy and return to a high vibrational track.

I've noticed that three consistent signs show up when energy starts to sink. If you notice one or more, it's time to recalibrate with a vibe-raising activity. The beauty of energy work is that frequencies can be controlled like a radio dial. Energy is always oscillating, so if you don't like your frequency, you can change the channel and find one that you do like. You should also take a minute to examine what caused your energy to dip in the first place and resolve the issue before it feeds a block or becomes one.

The first sign that your vibration is dipping is that your emotions are in the toilet. Anxiety, shame, fear, inadequacy, hopelessness, abandonment . . . these negative feelings come from a place of fear and can become a problem if you slosh around in them. It's okay to feel sad or angry, and unrealistic to think you should act or feel positive 24/7, but now that you get the damaging frequency that these emotions put out, make sure you don't linger there. Choose an activity that sparks joy, and then process what caused these feelings and peacefully let them go.

The second sign that your vibe is low is that you'll attract people with predominantly negative feelings—and their actions, words, and core values will drain you. Don't cut them out of your life (unless they're incredibly toxic) but do set boundaries like we discussed earlier. You can also use one of your activities to lift your energy or imagine wrapping the person in a pink bubble of love and sending them off into the heavens. Otherwise, you'll spend hours doing salt baths, dancing, and going for walks, which is a lot of time used to cope with just one person! Again, figure out what you're doing or saying that attracts these lower vibrational people to your words or lifestyle and what habits you might want to tweak so that they come around less often.

The final sign is that a lot of problems and crummy opportunities are dropping in your lap. You might feel suddenly overwhelmed by money problems or feel the weight of your work bogging you down. You sprain your ankle at the gym and that anniversary cruise to Hawaii gets canceled due to a norovirus outbreak. To turn your ship around, do one of your activities and remind yourself of who truly you are. Remember your Godliness and that lifting your energy is within your control. Always take a moment to consider why you've attracted this chaos at all.

Beyond these three signs, you'll feel like you're smack in the eye of a bad-luck tornado. Appliances break, your kids have problems at school, a family member gets sick, the Wi-Fi goes out. . . . What's funny is that my dogs are affected by energy dips too. One time an old friend of mine, who has a lot of self-created problems and tends to be energetically heavy, came to visit. I knew it wasn't a hot idea, but I wanted to catch up for old time's sake. Boy, did my dogs hate this choice. They had diarrhea all over the house, which is so odd because they're well trained. From this point on, their loose bowels became one of the many signs that my frequency was in danger. Dogs are energetic beings and can easily feel dips, so they purge.

FEELING LOW? TRY A HIGHER-SELF MEDITATION

If your energy needs a lift and/or you need help understanding why it dipped at all, a higher-self meditation can help. Here, you connect with a version of your soul that (1) fills you with pristine energy and (2) has already figured out the answers to some of your questions. I believe that while you are living on a present timeline, there are also multiple past, present, and future timelines that simultaneously exist in the universe. Although you have free will in all lifetimes, speaking with your higher self can help you gain insight. This is because the higher version of you is aware of—and has already been through—some version of the problems you're experiencing now. Spending time with your higher self may be all it takes to return your energy to an elevated frequency. It can also reveal new insight, feelings, thoughts, and healing paths for you to take.

Your higher self exists in a vibratory field beyond earth and is not influenced by past programming or worldly creations. Just being in the presence of your higher self is an environment that's rich with data. You don't even need to have a conversation with this version of you. Some of my clients complain that their higher self doesn't verbally communicate with them, but it's enough to bask in its presence and download the energy of this edifying creation. It fills you with answers when you need them.

To access your higher self, you must be in at least a neutral vibration to reach it. Jumping from an emotional collapse to divine wisdom is too high of a vibrational jump to make—and if you can, it's a roll of the dice and unsustainable. To hit neutral, it might be enough to take a few breaths, go for a run, vent to a friend to release your frustrations, or laugh at old YouTube videos of *The Tonight Show* to get yourself to a calmer and more centered mindset.

Now imagine a colored light (I like to use purple) coming from the sky and filling you up. Once you're full, follow the purple light like a laser back up to the sky, above the earth, and as high as you can go. Here, you'll bask in God's energy and light as if you're on the beach on a sunny day. When you're ready, gently coast back down to earth. I don't communicate with my higher self or other celestial beings here. I believe that if you can tap into God's energy, it will transmute the thoughts, solutions, and gifts that you have yet to acquire to your future self. At the end of this visualization, ask your higher self for answers. Now it will provide them.

TWIN PEAKS: LOVE AND SURRENDER

The highest frequencies you can reach are love and surrender—so when your vibration needs a boost, serving others with love or surrendering to a higher power will surely lift or return your frequency to its highest point. Existing on such an elevated level also shines a spotlight on whether you are living your human story or divine story. When you're living your human story, you are limited; but when you embody your divine story, you are limit*less*. Your human story includes all your limits like trauma, illness, heartbreak, and debt. But your divine story is about your gifts, creation, and your highest self. When you focus on living your divine story, it's about love, potential, creation, and newness; this makes your human story feel secondary, or maybe even irrelevant at times, don't you think? If you ask me, living your divine story is a revelatory and high vibrational way to move through the world with grace and glory to God. Both stories are available to you. You can even create a vision board that reminds you of your divine story's achievements to keep you on track. Here, you'll post reminders of when you received a lesson, noticed a sign, and witnessed a miracle—in other words, when your divine story manifested itself in real life. This isn't a board about what you want to create in the future; it's a reminder and *proof* that the universe provides and, even on earth, honors the divine in you.

Love comes in many forms. It can look like gratitude, connection, forgiveness, empathy, or love felt. So I do my best to fill my life with people and opportunities that embody love as best they can. My babysitters, friends, employees—they're all openhearted and loving souls. This helps the overall frequency in our home and business stay high and avoid lower emotions like fear, shame, anger, sadness, and rage. Of course, it's impossible to avoid some of these feelings when I'm serving as a healer, teacher, or spiritual activator because I tend to feel what others feel—especially their pain. But when this happens, I know how to clear and raise my energy back up. I also find that when I don't surround myself with love, things move at a slower pace. It takes longer to solve problems, fix health issues, create new projects—life slogs along.

Before I led workshops of my own, I worked closely with Mandy to produce, market, and generally help with hers. I remember a woman named Jennifer, a regular at Mandy's events, who brought her friend Betsy to a workshop with the hope that Mandy could help her. Betsy was suicidal, which worried me for obvious reasons. I knew this student would be an especially big challenge for us. Poor Betsy had been through a lot. She'd dealt with an abusive partner for years who was in and out of jail, had a chronic autoimmune illness, was recently fired from her job, fought depression, had seen a therapist for 25 years, was on heavy meds—and had already written her suicide letter when she came to see us. Betsy felt like she had nothing left to live for, and I could feel this woman's pain. I rarely see this much defeat in a student's face and soul. But we agreed to try to help her; what's the worst that could happen?

Betsy's detox did not go as I expected—in a good way. I'd mapped out a plan in my mind to get Betsy back on track, because the stakes were so high. On Day 1, Mandy and I simply spent time with Betsy, getting to know her and the others at the workshop. On this first day, we typically pump as much love into the environment and our students as we can. Then on Day 2—before we could even start our tactical lessons—Betsy cracked a smile. The color returned to her face, and she openly shared her story. Betsy said that she felt healed, and I knew that as unbelievable as it sounds, this turnaround manifested from love frequency alone. I'd never seen anything like it! On Day 3, we all spent the day reveling in each other's company and new friendship. When I asked Betsy what helped her change course so quickly, sure enough, she credited the unconditional love she felt emanating from Mandy. Betsy said that her mother rarely demonstrated love toward her, but Mandy's love helped glue all her broken pieces back together. My jaw always drops then I witness how love makes such quick, dramatic inroad with blocks.

Embodying the energy of love jump-starts transformation, because it opens and works with your heart chakra, the most powerful energy field in your body. It raises your vibration while affecting your crown chakra to allow loving intuition to flow. And when you actively show love, you serve from the highest good. You perform selfless acts with emotional intensity, and you can make the most of that state. You can demonstrate love with a good deed or demonstrate and transfer that feeling to another person's company. While some open their heart best by donating to a charity, others might do it by making a meal for a loved one or connecting with someone in need. I'm filled with a warm, fuzzy feeling when I'm serving in a workshop or group setting. Mandy can simply sit with another person, and they will feel her overwhelming love.

Surrender is your other frequency game changer—and its incredibly high frequency emanates from your willingness to give yourself to a higher power and submit to what's holding you back. Your action step here is actually no action step; it's an emotional, internal shift that you make in your mind. When you realize that you don't have all the answers you crave, you surrender the problem and put it in God's hands. At that point, you follow whatever signs God lays out to lead you to the highest good. Set the intention, "God, I don't know all the answers, and I'm asking for help." This intention moves mountains. To give up on trying to control what you can't—and handing it to the superior energy in our universe—allows you to step out of the way so God can determine what's next, and best, for you. Rest in the vibration of trust and faith.

Giving your problem to God and then waiting for direction isn't a lazy way to deal with a problem. It isn't about giving up, either. You must do the work of following clues that appear in the real world or pings to your heart and instincts. Once you receive signs, you must jump on them, knowing that your mind isn't leading but that a higher power is. God's signs can happen an hour, a few days, or even a week later. Surrendering to this process has never let me down.

Since love and surrender vibrate so high, Mandy and I tap into both when we have a tough problem or emotional issue to overcome. Love, as I've mentioned, is a no-brainer and simply requires reaching inward to serve and care for others. Surrender is a whole other ball game. We used to practice this as a last resort after running in circles with nothing left to give, but lately, we strive to make surrender *a first step* so that God is fully in charge of our process from the start. Of course, this is easier said than done. Emotions, expectations, our monkey minds, and need for control can get in the way. Nonetheless, our intentions sound like this: "God, I'm so lost. Please guide me to my next steps. I am open. I'm laying it down. I'm in over my head and need your help." We set them with humility, vulnerability, and sincerity—the more real emotion, the better. This connects us to the universe from a deep and true heart space.

MAKING HIGH ENERGY A LIFESTYLE

In no time at all, raising and maintaining energy will become a way of life. And when you raise and maintain your vibration, factors that would have caused it to lower start to show themselves, so that you can avoid or remove them before they turn into challenging blocks. At this high vibration, you'll also feel sensitive around situations that run contrary to your new values and priorities. Your body will always want to return to its best vibration—and the people or situations that don't belong there will feel uncomfortable and foreign. Best of all, scenarios that once frustrated you won't have the same emotional charge that they once did. You won't even crave drama anymore. In so many words, you're reborn and every part of you knows it.

A few years ago, my client Sue came to me to privately help her raise her vibration. She told me that she'd felt stuck in a low vibrational state for a while and had attracted a boyfriend who was both cheating on her and treating her poorly in general. As I worked on Sue, I sensed that she and her boyfriend were, in fact, still together because their low vibrations were drawn to each other. After helping Sue raise her vibe, I suggested that she have her boyfriend come see me so that I could work with him as well to encourage greater compatibility. Sue didn't want to leave her partner outright, so she liked the suggestion. All that said, after driving six hours to see me, Sue's boyfriend couldn't even enter our high vibrational home because he said that just being near it made him uncomfortable, anxious, and afraid! Instead, he chose to turn around and drive back home, without a healing—even outside our house! It reminded me of how someone with a bad conscience might feel uncomfortable entering a church because their vibrations don't match the environment. We emit energy from our fields, and if they're not similar, they can't co-exist. In the end, Sue broke up with her guy and, shortly after, met a new man that she happily married. Their vibrations and ambitions not only match but encourage each other to be their best.

Like Sue and so many others, when you move through the world with a sparkling vibration, your normal changes for the better. You feel brighter, happier, and fueled by divine energy and not human priorities. Use this creation energy to blast through obstacles. It is the power of you and God united—a bold and beautiful energy in its purest form. When you embody this frequency, it feeds your soul, heals blocks, and prevents future ones from forming.

In the next chapter, you will—drum roll, please—discover and explore your unique supernatural gifts. This is one of the most exciting parts of my detox—the part that makes my students giddy with anticipation. Gifts are so special and tied to your purpose, as they provide you with clarity, direction, and guide you toward the highest good. So without further ado . . .

More Resources and Free Downloads

I've put together a powerful daily checklist called "21 Ways You Can Raise Your Vibration Quickly." Download it here:
www.SpiritualActivator.com/raiseyourvibe

Chapter 6

DAYS 10–12: DISCOVER YOUR GIFTS

AS AUTHOR MARK TWAIN is often quoted as saying, "The two most important days in your life are the day you are born, and the day you find out why." This is where your spiritual gifts come in. Our spiritual gifts are given to us so that we thrive in this lifetime and heartfully serve others for the greatest good of all. Our gifts are also directly linked to our purpose work, which we'll discuss more deeply in the next chapter, but for now, know that you should never get caught up in wanting your service to "look" a certain way. A monk called to meditate on top of a mountain for 20 years can have the same vibrational impact as a person who smiles at a depressed stranger or generous parent who tutors children after school.

Every one of us has been given one or more spiritual gifts—and yes, I'm talking supernatural abilities. And even though this is a surprising concept to imagine—*me? a psychic or healer?*—your gifts are unfolding so that you can use them for a higher purpose, and never with the intention to hurt or cause harm. It's a good idea to start using them on friends and family until you feel comfortable enough with your abilities that you embody them and serve without hesitation. What's most important to know is that your gifts have been revealed, and will unfold and grow, at the perfect place and time. You've been granted divinely crafted abilities so that your soul can honor and respect God's gifts and use them to make the world a better place.

All gifts are delineated in a soul contract that you sign before incarnating to this lifetime and body. And while your gifts are specific to the lessons and purpose work you're tasked to pursue, you may also have had different gifts from past lifetimes that you can tap into now. Together, your gifts will join forces so that you have the abilities you need. For instance, if you were a psychic in a past life and a healer in this one, having both at your disposal will make you better at your purpose work. As a hands-on healer with psychic abilities, you can determine where an illness comes from, if it's influenced by trauma, and when it will run its course. This levels up a healing gift that solely allows you to remove blocks and illness from a body. That said, you will explore only your primary gift in this book. Future gifts, whether they are new or from past lives, will likely appear at a later date and when you're energetically ready.

Your gift is a vehicle for spreading hope, mercy, faith, compassion, and generosity. You have spiritual jobs on this planet, and by using your abilities, God wants you to form a devoted community that loves, enlightens, and helps others move through their lives with purpose and empowerment. We will explore how to use your gifts for purpose work in the next chapter. For now, you will simply discover the primary gift you'll use to make everyone's human experience, including yours, more peaceful to navigate. After all, we live in a difficult world that's riddled with heartache, illness, selfishness, pride, anger, grief, shame, guilt, fear, and other experiences and emotions that deplete us and understandably lower vibrations. Leaning in to gifts that make life more joyful and meaningful will sprinkle a little sunshine on the struggles we face every day.

In this chapter, we'll discuss when to explore your gifts during this detox, why your gifts are only accessible on certain vibrations, and how your gifts have given you clues that they've been part of your soul all along. You'll then read about the six gifts that I see most often in my workshops and decide which you possess—complete with a meditation to clear any confusion. This is such a fun part of the work I do. Get excited! Your spiritual gifts are ready to meet you!

WHEN TO EXPLORE YOUR GIFTS

During Days 10–12, you will focus on understanding and familiarizing yourself with your primary gift, though *you will not practice it until the final three days of your detox*, discussed in the next chapter. At this point in the program, I'd like you to continue practicing your morning, evening, and optional impromptu practices as you discover your primary gift. It's important to continue this routine at this time, so that the whole shebang becomes habitual and feels natural. I want your overall detox routine to really stick so that you can continue growing and knowing what it feels like to develop and live in your own genuine energy.

On Day 10, I'd like you to review the six spiritual gifts in this chapter and figure out which best describes you. Notice how you feel as you read each description. Does your stomach get butterflies? Do you feel overwhelming peace and love? Do you feel excited or "seen"? Does your gut tell you that certain gifts are just what you need to begin the next chapter of your life? Again, choose the gift that resonates most. If you identify with more than one, I've included a meditation at the end of the chapter to help you determine the order in which to pursue them.

On Day 11, after you've embraced your gift, please examine how your past has been hinting at this gift all along. This isn't just an amusing activity but an eye-opening exercise that reinforces faith in your soul's plan and helps you trust your future path, plus the guardian angels and other souls that guide you. Ask yourself: What activities have you been most drawn to? Who in your community is the most influential and inspiring to you? What have you done in the past that has used aspects of this gift? Have others complimented you about your gift's traits?

On Day 12, you're going to rest. Determining your gifts can be emotionally and spiritually exhausting. Take the day to process what you've learned, and let this new information settle and integrate with your consciousness. Take a walk, run a bubble bath, or snuggle with a pet. You've pivoted into an exciting new reason to wake up in the morning and be your best.

GIFTS SURFACE ONLY ON THE RIGHT VIBE

Exploring your gifts is the next sensible step in your detox, after working hard to elevate and sustain a high vibration, since you can only access the best version of your gifts when your energy is high and strong. A gift's performance is vibrationally based, so the higher your energy, the stronger and easier it is to access. You can tap into gifts on a lower vibration, but you'll only be able to use rudimentary skills and low vibrational energy (for example, if you're a channel or psychic, and your energy vibrates with feelings of shame, you'll tap into spirits that exist on a similarly low frequency). This will also happen if you take illegal drugs on a regular basis or feel negative emotions like shame, anger, and apathy, which live on a lower frequency. On the other hand, raising your energy unlocks stronger and more exciting frequency levels that let you experience your gift in mature ways. The higher your vibe, the more illuminating your gifts.

The universe intends for you to use your gifts as a spiritual GPS—a navigation system that you tune in to every day that will guide you toward your best life. When you allow energy to clearly flow through you as you use these abilities, particularly after a detox, it naturally raises your vibration and points you toward awakening. Your intuition is also strongest when you use it to work with your gifts. When I embraced my spiritual gifts, my life flipped on its head. I went from feeling blue and directionless most days to feeling chosen and purposeful. I flowed and existed, every day, at a naturally high vibration. I loved serving and felt guided all the time.

CONNECTING THE DOTS

Once you review the gift descriptions below and recognize the ones that feel most like you, your mind will have an immediate *aha* moment. It will then begin to automatically scan your past and consider intuitive pulls, career choices, dreams, illnesses, and impactful moments that feel thematically tied to your gifts. The universe has dropped clues to help you recognize this since you were born, but only now are you ready to connect the dots from the past to the present—particularly with your passions or line of work. If you're a professional health writer, you may be a channeler or healer. If you're a counselor, you could be a transmuter. As you read the gift descriptions in a bit, you'll start to recognize how your strengths relate to your gifts.

Though we're all innately born with gifts, some of us turn them off at an early age. It might have felt painful or scary to consider having these, due to social constraints. Or, perhaps as a child, you saw a spirit and it freaked you out. You might have also worried that your family would wrongly assume you were dabbling in the occult. I've heard this from clients all over the world—from the Bible Belt in the Southern United States to Catholic countries like Brazil or the Philippines. Even so, I believe that condemnation comes from those who need to feel certainty in their lives or have control over others; their judgment has nothing to do with your soul. But I get why you'd feel pressure to conform to the environment around you. I was the same way. The good news is that you carry gifts not just from lifetime to lifetime, but also from bloodline to bloodline. This means you'll be very understanding if your own kids share your abilities.

Because gifts are a divine part of your soul, stifling them can create havoc in your energetic system. It's like plugging your nose or wearing a bandana over your eyes; you are meant to use these body parts to function in the world, so without them, it's hard to adapt. God also really wants you to use your spiritual gifts, so if you don't, there is kickback. For instance, you might get headaches or feel intense, chronic anxiety. You might find that the weather swings to extremes, or that your electricity goes haywire.

You might also get rashes or feel body aches that your doctors can't explain. A student of mine named Jake discovered his hands-on healing abilities during one of my detox workshops. And while he practiced it after leaving, he didn't stick with it because he didn't put boundaries around how much others demanded from him. A few months into his practice, he felt so overwhelmed with appointments that he stopped healing. He also stopped talking about his gift and assumed he could ignore it like he did before he began using his gift full time. Abruptly halting his energetic flow did not bode well for Jake's body.

Months later, Jake called me in tremendous pain, begging for a healing. He told me he felt like he'd been "hit by a train." Jake was only in his early 40s, yet it felt to me that he had the brittle bones of an old man. He walked with a limp. I could feel that his muscles and joints were like Jell-O, seemingly mushy and easily falling apart. Jake stayed overnight with us, but because it was so painful for him to make the stairs, he gave up halfway and slept on our staircase! Jake said doctors were at a loss and had no real solutions for his misery—his labs and test results were normal. Immediately, I knew the reason for Jake's pain was because he stopped using his healing gift. I asked him to pursue his purpose again and insisted he start not with me healing him, but by him doing a healing on Mandy to remove energy blocks. Well, I kid you not: after the healing, *all* of Jake's pain disappeared within minutes. Every ache and pain in his body was stagnant energy! This is not the first time I've seen this, but it is one of the most extreme cases for sure.

A Quick Word about Gifts

Investigating your gifts shouldn't feel difficult or forced, so have fun with the exploratory process. You're tapping into a *supernatural ability* that's going to change your life! Get pumped! Now developing your gift does take some work, but only to an extent. You'll need to care for your energetic body by regularly cleansing and enjoying self-care so you don't become drained or overwhelmed by others' toxic energy. You'll also need to practice your gift but not stress about it, as if you're grooming an entirely new skill set. It won't feel like learning to play the trombone in third grade. Your gift is *familiar* to your soul, so learning how to use it will feel natural and become an unconscious competence, a psych term that refers to when someone has had so much practice with a skill that it's now become second nature and can be done easily.

IT'S TIME TO OPEN YOUR GIFTS!

In my classes, I personally help students determine their gifts, but by using this book, you're relying on your own intuition to guide you, which is frankly preferable because you're exercising your gut instincts and faith in divine guidance. Knowing your primary gift is a sacred awareness. Give thanks to God, your higher power, or your angels—and be grateful that you were given your gift and purpose work on this planet, for this lifetime, and perhaps others to come.

Below, I've described six abilities that are telltale signs of spiritual gifts. Reflect on how each description makes you feel as you read, and feel free to circle or check the qualities that best describe you. Are there more than six gifts in the world? Of course! Projectors, for instance, house energy for multitudes of people and turn thoughts into things very quickly. There are also spiritual activators, like me, who flick on a person's spiritual abilities like a light switch. Even so, I'm deliberately not including more than six gifts in this chapter, since others require more of a spiritual foundation than the ones we are building via our detox. Plus, they often come to clients as more advanced, secondary gifts, so there's no need to get into them now.

If you feel drawn to multiple abilities out of the gate, please meditate on which resonate most with you by using the exercise at the end of this chapter. Put the others on a back burner until you're comfortable using your main gift and get signs from the universe that you're ready to move on. Most students practice one gift for 30 to 90 days before investigating others.

Here are the six primary gifts that I most often see in students. They all require practice plus routines to establish spiritual boundaries, energetic safety, and precision. I teach a lot of this at workshops, but I've also created a resource page at AuthenticLiving.com to get you started.

A CHANNEL

About a quarter of my students are channels. Channeling is a very special gift that allows you to communicate with divine sources of energy like spirit guides, light beings, archangels, and God energy through your crown chakra, which is located at the top of your head. This powerful chakra allows you to receive divine messages and access higher levels of consciousness.

Channels obtain information for the highest good of all. The quality of their messages relies on the channeler's vibration, and believe it or not, has nothing to do with the frequency of the person they're reading. Like all gifts, the more you practice your ability and the higher your vibration, the faster you will channel, the more info you'll access, and the more enlightened your messages will be. You will deliver only messages that the sitter needs to receive at that time.

Channels have been said to bring new information to the world to enlighten the masses. German physicist Albert Einstein and, before him, the ancient Greek philosopher Aristotle are rumored to have been channelers. Aristotle made such significant contributions to so many categories of human knowledge—including physics, religion, astronomy, biology, metaphysics, dreams, politics, economics, logic, ethics, poetry, theater, music, and psychology—that many spiritual teachers insist that his awareness must have been pulled from a brilliant divine source. He also wrote extensively on the state of a living being's soul. Einstein, too, was a relatively spiritual man, interested in the cosmos and what made the universe tick. Today, many believe that most writers are channelers, and that some fiction writers tell stories that are subconsciously gathered from the universe's collective unconscious or from a past or parallel lifetime.

When I teach a workshop, some of my past graduates like to help—a bit like a TA or right-hand man, so to speak. They enjoy serving students and passing on what they've learned. When this happens, the students' gifts seem to activate more potently than if I were teaching alone—and the graduates' gifts do the same, since they're serving a high cause, which makes their vibration shoot through the roof. One time, my graduate Leslie, whose primary gift is to channel, suddenly began speaking in light language in the middle of a lecture. If you've never heard of this, light language is the language of the soul. It can sound like gibberish, a foreign language (similar to speaking in tongues), or even the sound dolphins make. That day, Leslie's language mirrored that of dolphins, which are known to be highly evolved animals. Some believe their tones and sounds maintain our world's balance of energy and support humans on their journeys. I just know it sounded cool. After tapping into this language, Leslie channeled messages from a hidden archangel (an archangel that isn't as popular as those in the Bible). Here, her voice changed again—it was lower, deeper, and slower than usual. *The class was in awe!*

I encourage channelers to reach the highest vibration you can access. Newbies love channeling angels and archangels, since they're such gentle and highly evolved beings of love. If you resist the information coming through, you'll likely feel chronic anxiety or a "channeler's hangover," which includes brain fog, headaches, and low energy. You must hear and deliver messages to feel relief and ensure that your physical, mental, and energetic bodies feel balanced.

You might be a channel if . . .

- You like to spend time alone and find that solitude recharges your batteries

- You crave chocolate, sweets, and alcohol to relax

- You have so much excess energy that you feel anxious or want to move your body

- You have a lot of wisdom for your age and have always said profound things

A TRANSMUTER

A transmuter cleanses energy for others. Simply by sitting next to another person, maybe by having a conversation with them, the transmuter can clear the other person's negative energy. Think of transmuters as air purifiers for energy. Transmuters attract negative people, because they help them feel better; they naturally cleanse and neutralize their energy like a filter. The result is that one person feels amazing relief because they've been cleansed of toxic feelings, while the transmuter feels like a full or clogged filter in need of changing. Subsequently, transmuters must keep their energy high and regularly cleanse to keep their health and mood intact. Transmuters can even cleanse energy for an entire city, state, or planet! Mandy is an incredible transmuter and has been known to clear toxic energy for miles. The last time she did this, she was in Miami, and the city's energy felt dark and negative to her. She was intuitively pulled to stand on the balcony of our rental and hold the palm of one hand facing the ocean and the palm of her other hand facing the city. In doing so, she transmuted *the entire city's* toxic energy and sent it into the ocean to be washed away by Mother Earth. After, Mandy sat down to rest, as her entire body shook, and she cried. This is how she cleared the energy from her body.

My student Jonathan is a transmuter too. When we first met, he was overweight and looked burned out. He cried a lot. I could tell from his appearance, demeanor, and energy that he was a transmuter, since they're very sensitive, feel easily overwhelmed, and tend to carry extra weight for energetic protection. They have very big hearts and a love/hate relationship with humanity—in other words, they're drawn to help people, but also feel like people take advantage of their energy. Transmuters are the friends you go to when you need to vent or solve a problem. Moms often fall into this role as the "fixer" of their family's problems. People pleasers, those who have trouble saying no, and those who hesitate to establish boundaries with friends and family fall into this group too. Sometimes they're so sensitive that they can't watch horror films or brutal news reports, because they absorb the characters' and subjects' negative experiences.

Transmuters often mistake their gift for a character flaw and seek therapy. Here, they can learn to create better boundaries, but they can never turn off their generous gift. Though transmuters sound a lot like empaths, empaths only feel what others do, while transmuters actually absorb another's energy and cleanse it from their energetic body to help that person find balance. Transmuters feel and act as if the emotions are theirs—it's very heavy work.

Transmuters need to spend more time cleansing and raising their energy than most. When you are dealing with your own intense stress, plus that of others, your energy can become very dense. Solitude, self-care, and cleansing practices are essential. Connecting to a higher power helps manage your energy and receive spiritual fuel too. And if you can vibrate on a consistent love frequency, you will transmute better, faster, and won't take on as much from others. If you don't clear your heavy energy, you may nap or snack a lot with grounding food like alcohol, sugar, or chocolate. You may even eat just like the person you're transmuting for. Transmuting can feel like a thankless job sometimes, but it is a deep gift since you're constantly serving others' energetic bodies. And unlike channeling, it doesn't always require a conscious effort.

I'll never forget a very mushy, in love, and engaged couple named Laura and Gary who came to see me. As I walked this duo through their detox, his wife felt incredible—full of energy, tremendous relief, and stress free. Meanwhile, Gary became sick as a dog. He was sneezing, throwing up, had diarrhea—if there was a hole in his body, he purged from it. Gary was clearly a transmuter, so as his fiancée removed all her blocks, he absorbed them for her to the point that his overwhelmed body had to drain and expel them! Once they were both block-free and had released their toxins, Gary didn't have to worry about this happening as much, because Laura's initial toxic load was now gone. I can only imagine what their marriage—and any future pregnancies—will be like! When Mandy was pregnant with Zion, she didn't experience a difficult pregnancy—but I did. I underwent a sympathetic pregnancy, which is when a woman's partner has symptoms that mimic pregnancy. It was chock full of morning sickness, nausea, weight gain, and insomnia. I even felt tiny kicks in my belly when the baby would kick Mandy! This mostly went away after Mandy's first trimester, but I was happy to share this energetic bond with my wife and clear some of her less pleasant symptoms for her. And hey, I'm not alone. Men have been transmuting for their pregnant wives for centuries! In fact, many cultures have ritualized this. The Cantabri people, a pre-Roman civilization that lived during the second half of the first millennium BC, had a custom where a father, during or immediately after a child's birth, went to bed, complained of labor pains, and was given treatments usually reserved for women during and after childbirth. And in Papua New Guinea, fathers once built huts outside their villages, where they'd experience and mimic labor pains until their infant was born.

You might be a transmuter if . . .

- People love being around you and say they feel better when you're together
- You're a go-to for wise, helpful, and feel-good advice
- You feel drained after a conversation, whether it's in person or on the phone
- Just being in busy environments like malls and crowded cities exhausts you
- Self-care, cleansing, and vibration-raising techniques help you recharge

A PSYCHIC

Psychics tap into energetic frequencies (crystal balls and tarot cards, optional). They have an innate "sense of knowing" that yields thoughtful insight into the people and world around them. Psychics download information in dreams and via visions that come to fruition; they have a general awareness of how the past and present will play out. They can help solve crimes, usher stuck spirits into the light, remote view, and help business tycoons improve their work instincts.

A few years ago, I remember that I had a class full of psychics galore. There isn't typically one dominant gift that overpowers the others, but for this workshop, God really had a thing for psychics. Class began with various students finishing each other's sentences and sharing visions that came to pass. One woman dreamed of a student's face before her first class and recognized her immediately. Another budding psychic connected with the Lemurian realm, where it's said that a highly evolved spiritual race encourages oneness and healing. Others saw auras for the first time, and a few simultaneously communicated with a spirit named Travis, who apparently lives in our retreat center. At one point, a student saw an eagle—a symbol of strength, inspiration, guidance, and majesty—fly out of Mandy's mouth and watched me transform into a bear—a symbol of thoughtfulness, strength, family, courage, and strong will in the spiritual traditions of Native Americans. The energetic exchange at that workshop was on fire!

As a psychic, it's important to establish boundaries with the spirit world so *you* are in charge of the information that flows through you and ensure that it comes from a divine source of love and light and is for the highest good of all. Do know, however, that when messages come through, they're meant to be shared, and your audience should take prompt action.

Mediums can also have psychic abilities, though not all psychics are mediums. Mediums mostly channel messages from the other side, including the deceased, who with a person's spirit guides, can relay the future. If a medium pulls messages from their third eye, they use psychic skills and deliver more humanistic info like the birth of a child or an impending car accident. If the messages come from their higher self, angels, or God, however, they're channeling through the crown chakra, which is what makes you pull positive, and higher level, thoughts and guidance.

You might be a psychic if . . .

- You often experience déjà vu
- You know things without anyone telling you
- When you touch people or objects, you sense information about them

- You see or feel spirits and other beings, and/or sense different realms of sacred knowledge
- Your dreams come true when you're awake

Dream a Little Dream for Me

When you open to your spiritual gifts, dreams become more than a passing experience while you're snoozing. They tend to carry a deep meaning, since you're now vibrating on a higher frequency. I suggest keeping a notebook and pen on your nightstand to jot down your dreams and revisit them in the morning. When you review the dreams, it's okay if they don't make sense at first. Many times, you're processing or channeling energy during your dreams, and their meanings aren't intended to be as literal as you'd like. Write the narratives down anyway. In time, I promise they will come together to unveil one or more *aha* moments.

Dreams can reveal so much about your life and those in it. When you dream, try to pick up on patterns and synchronicities that play out when you're awake. If you notice recurring animals, symbols, or objects, you can look them up in a dream dictionary, page through an online resource, or view their meaning through your own lens. God personalizes the signs in my dreams. They pair with symbols that I receive when I'm awake, so that all the signs collectively guide me. It's important to understand how your mind, soul, and higher self use dreams as part of your journey in this lifetime. No matter what, I've never met a person who's realized their gifts and then never had dreams that carry deeper meaning—they may just present themselves in different ways, depending on how your soul prefers to download spiritual information.

You can also dream of yourself in other timelines, universes, and alternate realities. I'm shown there's more than one universe in the cosmos, and all universes are slightly different. Within these universes are parallel worlds—and alternate versions of us. So during dreams, I believe you can astral travel to these universes or even to different locations within your current universe. I often dream of myself as a surgeon, so I believe this is my life on another timeline.

To astral travel, it helps to massage your third eye and crown chakra at the same time, for about a minute. Do this before bed, or even better, before a nap so that you don't fall into too deep of a sleep and stay alert to where your soul is, relative to your body. (For more info on how to safely astral travel, go to AuthenticLiving.com). After the first time I did a healing on Mandy's mom, her soul astral traveled in the middle of the night to our bedroom! Mandy saw her consciousness standing over me with a smile. Mandy's mom didn't remember doing this, so it wasn't deliberate, but Mandy remembers reaching out to touch her mom because she looked so real that she thought she was sleep walking! Mandy's hand passed through her like a hologram.

Finally, you may experience lucid dreaming. This is a bit like astral travel, but it's a dream in which your mind is aware that you're dreaming. It can feel like your soul is hovering above the dream, as if watching and/or commenting on the dream like it's a movie. You've likely had a lucid dream during a nightmare, when your mind kicked in and forced you to wake up.

If you're a transmuter, you can dream about someone else's life—which will subconsciously prompt you to cleanse that person's energy, even when you're sound asleep. About 10 years ago, Mandy and I stayed at an Airbnb in Dallas while running a workshop. At night, Mandy dreamed we were fighting about subjects that didn't make sense to us—and it turned out she was transmuting the energy of the woman who owned the apartment we were renting! She and her partner argued nonstop, and the owner had a lot of childhood trauma. When Mandy dreamed, she felt and cleansed it all. This was before Mandy understood how to establish boundaries around her gift, so she felt the woman's experiences on a deep and painful level. Luckily, Mandy did know how to cleanse and return to a happy and peaceful baseline.

Dreams take up a good portion of our lives, so frame them as a time to heal, lean on your gifts, soul travel, and learn. I'm proactive about how I use my sleep time and suggest you are too. Before bed, I set either a broad intention ("God, please reveal whatever is in the highest good for me to learn") or specific one ("I'd like to learn and experience forgiveness for the highest good of all. So be it.") about what I'd like to experience. I like to use my eight hours to process, communicate, and work with God and my higher self. I love it when I download information as I sleep, understand lessons in a parallel life, and receive messages from my higher self about what I need to improve in this life so that I can manifest or chase my goals once I'm awake.

I also appreciate when God helps me learn lessons in dreams, so I don't have to do it in my waking life. Recurring dreams often serve this purpose too; it might be too painful to repeatedly face a lesson while you're awake, so your guides may ask you to pay attention to it while you're asleep. This happened to my friend Marie, who after her divorce, had a recurring dream about hanging out with her ex before they parted ways. In the dreams, he was consistently indifferent, and she, uncharacteristically needy. It wasn't until Marie set the intention for this dream to end and mentally cut cords before going to sleep, that the dream stopped. She realized her angels were teaching her that she'd never get what she emotionally craved from her ex. This was a tremendous lesson for Marie about the importance of letting go and severing soul contracts. Dreams can act as divine feedback that contributes to spiritual growth. They happen for a reason.

HANDS-ON HEALERS

Hands-on healers have a natural, powerful, and uplifting energy that can resolve energetic blocks, plus emotional and physical illnesses, via touch or remotely (like over the phone or far away). Some healers can even transfer their energy into water for you to drink or cotton for you to tape to your body for healing purposes. Healers instinctively know where a person needs healing, either through a body scan similar to the one I taught you in Chapter 4, through mental or symbolic pictures in their mind's eye, or via sensations they feel in their own bodies that mirror their clients' issues. Many massage therapists and body workers have this gift and aren't conscious of it. I believe anyone can heal, to differing extents, if they master certain techniques.

Once a healer's energy is activated, their whole body— particularly their hands—carry energy that works miracles. A healer's hands become hot, tingle, feel magnetic, get pins and needles, and/or pulse. I activated the gift of a Colorado vet who healed her patients via touch. She'd diagnose their issue by instinct, run tests as needed, then heal them herself. She'd never talk about this with the owners. Healers who choose to work with animals are rare and super fascinating. They speak with animals verbally and telepathically, and just like many healers who work with humans, animal healers use their hands and intuition to scan for problems. In doing so, animal healers know what their "clients" think and feel on a very deep level. Most animal healers shine when it comes to resolving mystery illnesses and behavioral problems. They can even help give a pet closure when another animal in the household dies.

I've found that hands-on healers tend to know a lot about the body and medical world, because they have their own history of struggling with health issues; this gives them anecdotal context when working with a client's body. My student Faith is a perfect example of this. Before detoxing her energy, Faith agonized over multiple medical issues that she felt were from trapped traumas and negative emotions. In total, she'd suffered four strokes, sixteen back surgeries, and a brain injury—all of which led to 10 years of bedridden, chronic pain. While taking an online workshop, however, Faith heard a voice in her head that told her to move the energy in her daughter's back to help with pain—and when Faith did this, her daughter's pain disappeared! This told us that Faith was clearly a hands-on healer. The next morning, I did a healing and deeper activation on Faith, and 90 percent of her pain disappeared! Ever since, Faith has removed hundreds of blocks and healed clients of mental illness, cancer, kidney failure, and the like. She's really good at cluing in to their ailments and performing a kind of "psychic surgery" with her hands, because of her background and knowledge about bodily dysfunction.

Healers must be careful about how they protect and channel their energy. If they pull healing from their human energy, they will get tapped out. But if they receive it from a higher power, healing energy runs through their crown chakra, into their hands, and they always feel fortified. Using sacred geometry can also be a powerful tool (say, by imagining clients in a pyramid or diamond). This way, clients get a double dose of healing: from channeling energy and from the symbol. Finally, it's essential to protect yourself as a healer because you're working with someone else's energy, and you don't want to absorb their pain or emotions.

You might be a hands-on healer if . . .

- You feel other people's illness when you touch or are around them
- Your hands burn, tingle, pulse—and medical diagnoses have been ruled out
- You are intuitive when it comes to knowing the reason for, or how to fix, medical issues

- Past experiences have connected you to the medical field—either as a patient, caretaker, child of doctors or nurses, health editor or writer, etc.

- You have great love, compassion, and empathy for those who suffer

AKASHIC RECORDS READER

The Akashic Records are a psychic "library of information" that includes everything that's ever happened in the universe—life, death, natural tragedies, you name it. Think of it as a vast number of energetic imprints, a living vibrational field that stores all possible futures, the present, and the past. As your soul begins its life experience, a field of energy is released that records every thought, word, action, desire, and emotion in this library. They hold information about your soul's purpose, soul families, all your incarnations, karmic debts and ties to this lifetime, soul contracts, medical cures, soulmate information, life lessons—in other words, the highest vibrational information that exists in the universe. It's like an energetic Google.

The Akashic Records are guarded by a Record Keeper and your spirit guides, and those who have access to the records either channel this information directly or communicate with your higher self or a Record Keeper during a session. Though the records store vast amounts of information, what you receive is what you need at that time, not what you want to hear.

Those given access to the Akashic Records are deep thinkers with curious, analytical minds. They're your friends who always have answers to problems and constantly seek to deepen their knowledge, research hard topics, and discover the answers to life's big questions. Readers provide guidance to others, ask questions appropriately, and handle the information as it comes. Reading the Akashic Records is often a secondary gift for psychics and channelers. Because these records contain every thought, emotion, and experience that has ever happened to every soul that has ever existed, across space and time, this is meant to guide your overarching journey on earth. It's not necessarily where you turn to for trivial needs like building a business, discovering your path to wealth, or finding a new home. The information here is much higher than that and taps into life lessons, soul missions, and past life issues/karmic debts that influence your journey now.

I've also noticed that those with access to the Akashic Records have pure hearts. This is necessary to balance love and light when you're reading the records, so you can maintain a perspective on what's going on in this world and how it relates to a greater, universal message. When my student Jamie activated her Akashic gift, she got a glimpse of a space outside this galaxy. She saw various shapes before her and was brought to a table with ancient tablets and sacred geometry so she could grasp the Akashic world in visual form. It was beautifully validating but also overwhelming. This is intense knowledge, and you must have a certain reverence for sacred topics around life, death, gifts, catastrophes, earthquakes, and soul lessons.

My client Tiffanie puts her Akashic readings to very special use. Even before we met, Tiffanie always felt deeply connected to Mother Nature, and specifically the earth. Yet she never had context for this sensation and wanted to know more about her gifts, the information she innately channeled, and why she was so drawn to the ground. Growing up in the Mojave Desert in California, she often collected rocks and spent hours studying the earth. Tiffanie also felt drawn to salt—and its relationship to the ocean, food, and energy. After taking one of my workshops, Tiffanie learned that she was an Akashic Records reader—and wanted to combine the information she channeled with her love for salts. She began sourcing and blending salts from around the world, based on the Akashic information she heard and different chemical properties of the salts she used. Her clients soak in the salts, eat them, drink them, smell them—all depending on the Akashic message she receives for the greater good. Tiffanie even keeps a bowl of salts on her desk for herself so that she can rest her fingers in them when she's feeling stressed. Just having this bowl near her is very relaxing. Tiffanie has also created a set of chakra salts and intuition sprays for Authentic Living that sold out immediately. Are you surprised?

Tiffanie's process is fascinating. She first grounds herself and connects to the other person's energy to receive details about them. Directing her request at Gaia, the Greek goddess of Earth and mother of all life, Tiffanie sets the intention, "Please give this person what they need to feel better." She feels the person's needs—from emotional to health concerns—and senses which ingredients will bring the most comfort. Tiffanie keeps a full stock of materials on hand. Her first client was a fellow workshop attendee who didn't reveal what was upsetting her, but Tiffanie could feel the woman's grief in her chest and knew she needed relief from this sadness. Back in her hotel room, Tiffanie filled a glass jar with pink Himalayan salts, essential oils, magnesium flakes, and other intuitively sourced ingredients. She shared the mixture with her classmate and asked her to bathe in it. The next day, the woman told Tiffanie that in the tub, she collapsed into tears. It was a cathartic, healing moment that granted an incredible release.

You might be an Akashic Records Reader if . . .

- You tend to "just know" things
- You've been told you have a large heart and "busy" or thoughtful mind
- You have an overanalytical mind
- People have called you a "know it all"
- You love to learn
- You're really good at *Trivial Pursuit*!

WEATHER AND ELECTRONICS

A final—and frankly mind-boggling—rare gift that I've seen in 5 percent of my clients is the ability to affect the weather and electronics. Initially, this can happen unintentionally, but with practice, those who have this rare gift can control the weather or electronics deliberately and at will. For example, if they are listening to low vibe music along with 10 million other people at the same time, they can send loving energy through the radio and it will affect all those people. Many people get depressed on days when the sun isn't shining, so when someone can manipulate the weather, it could affect a lot of people. I believe this is very much a telepathic gift tied to emotional strength.

During a recent workshop, I was helping students with their gifts, category by category, and the process was taking longer than usual. I typically save weather and electronics for the end of the gift-revealing session since there are so few students who have this ability. An hour into the process, I noticed that the weather and electronics group was getting super grumpy. I instinctively looked outside and noticed that a perfectly sunny day had turned stormy, and the sky began to thunder. The weather gurus were pissed off! When I pointed this out, they laughed about the fact that they were feeling restless and anxious—and I explained that their feelings were controlling the weather outside our window. Once I finally worked with this group, I kid you not, the sun came back out and the blue skies remained peaceful and calm until sundown. The whole class witnessed this and was shocked at how fast the weather swung from one extreme to another.

Those who can control electronics are even more rare than the weather folks—they're about 2 percent of my students. My family, as a whole, can do this at times, but none of us have the ability to do it on our own or deliberately. When we experience a big life or energy shift like moving homes, forgiving a loved one, or stepping into purpose work more deeply, all the important electronics in our home go kaput. The maintenance light turns on in our cars, clocks stop working, our Wi-Fi goes out.

You might be able to control the weather and electronics if . . .

- You've noticed that the weather is bad when you're upset and sunny when you're happy
- Electronics flicker on and off in your presence
- All your tech breaks down when you're going through an emotional or spiritual shift
- Things seem to "glitch" in your presence

ID Your Primary Gift

Do you resonate with more than one gift and need an assist on which to focus on first? Try this exercise. Find a quiet space to take five deep, slow breaths. Set an intention like, "God, I set the intention to choose a primary gift that serves the highest good of all." Imagine a beam of white light shooting down from the heavens and into your body. Rub your hands together to create heat energy for fifteen seconds, then write all your gifts on different pieces of paper. Crumble them into balls. Next, move your hands over all the paper balls, and scan for any that feel hot, tingly, magnetic, or that you're drawn to. Make sure your hands precede your thoughts. Some choices will feel more intense than others. Once you choose your paper ball, open it to reveal your primary gift. Don't doubt or redo the process. Trust that your hands were divinely guided to this paper. Repeat the practice when the time is right to choose a second and third gift.

PUTTING IT ALL TOGETHER

Now that you know what your primary gift is, how do you feel? Are you psyched to start working with it? Remember, the first few times that you practice it after a detox can feel slightly uncomfortable. You might worry that people will think you're imagining it or that you aren't as naturally gifted as other intuitives you know. It might be tempting to run from your gift or unconsciously block yourself from using it once again. But please don't do this; trust that you are worthy of your gift and able to practice it to your fullest potential. You should feel so blessed, because you now know the work that God has intended for you. Your gift is part of your soul.

It is my hope that you finally feel relieved, at peace, and seen. Your detox has led you to discover your gifts, which can be used to co-create a new reality. It is never too late to explore and use your gift for the greater good, and in the next and final chapter, you will determine how to step into this intention so that you can serve humanity in a fulfilling and meaningful way.

More Resources and Free Downloads

I've put together a free 5-part video series called "Discover and Unlock Your 5 Spiritual Gifts Now." This video provides a deeper exploration of spiritual gifts including what they are, how they work, and how they can help you reach your goals, today. Download it here: www.SpiritualActivator.com/5gifts

Chapter 7

DAYS 13–15: PRACTICE YOUR ABILITIES AND PURPOSE WORK

YOU'VE MADE IT! YOU'VE reached the pot of gold at the end of your rainbow! This detox has cleared your most intense blocks and allowed your energy to flow, uninterrupted, in its most potent form—the way that the universe has always intended for you to experience it. You've also discovered your extraordinary gift, and it's time to practice your primary ability, integrate it into your purpose work, and use your supernatural powers to serve the world as only you can.

Can I get a *whoo-hoo?*

Everything you've done until now has helped you release your darkest blocks, boost negative frequencies, and elevate your energy. This allows you to experience the joy, lightness, and ease that come with high energy, plus a positive heart and mind. And when you practice your gift and fold it into your purpose work, your energetic output becomes even more potent. One of the great things about purpose work is that it holds you accountable for sustaining a consistently high frequency that not only feeds your gift but unlocks new aspects of it. Another important point about purpose work is that it isn't a weekend job or hobby that you do once a month to feel good about yourself. It's intended to be the main thrust of your life trajectory, the reason you were born and what you are meant to do during this lifetime. God wants your primary gift to consume you in a good way, and when its service dominates your thoughts and emotions, your vibe reaches its peak. All of this enlightenment will make you feel like you're walking on air.

As you cruise through life on a high frequency, serving others along the way, your world will change. At first, this shift may feel startling, but it's all for the highest good. Thank the universe for helping to make any discouraging relationships disappear. Opportunities that brought you down, projects that didn't inspire you, and other depleting scenarios that no longer match your vibration will either vanish or present themselves for *you* to work through. Triggers and tests will come into view for you to resolve too. (Did you think God would do *all* the work? You do live on a free-will planet where you must do your part.) When you do a juice cleanse, that detox can cause rashes and a runny nose that seem like bad side effects, but they're truly signs that your cleansed body is removing all the toxins that no longer serve it. The final days of your energy detox are similar. You're getting used to living on a high frequency, full of clarity and peace. Removing and healing from the people, situations, and environments that don't support your alignment may make you feel uncomfortable at first, but they are part of the process.

Keep your eyes and ears peeled for patterns, synchronicities, and signs that point to limiting beliefs that the universe wants you to clear during your final detox days. On Day 13 of my client Belinda's detox, she found herself in two situations, back-to-back, that triggered her insecurities and asked her to stand in her power with confidence and assurance. Talk about a sign. The first instance happened at her doctor's office, when a nurse questioned the validity of her complicated autoimmune illness. And then the next day, a good friend also implied that her symptoms were in her mind, since they were so unusual. At first, Belinda's heart felt like it would crack under the weight of so much judgment, but then she realized that this back-to-back pattern was the universe calling her to speak her truth rather than push her feelings down. On Day 14, Belinda sent e-mails to both the nurse and her friend, explaining the medical validity of her condition—but more importantly, insisting that she didn't have to justify her condition to anyone but doctors who were helping her heal. As a natural channel, Belinda's words flowed freely from her soul to the page. When Belinda told me the story, we both felt the energetic shift in Belinda's field from her newfound self-assurance. She'd removed the start of a block that raised her vibe and strengthened her self-esteem, spiritual gift, *and* auric field.

Clearing your energetic body, raising your frequency, and using your primary gift for the highest good are now central to daily life—which means (bonus!) that manifesting your desires will become faster and simpler too. Everything that's available on the frequency that you've achieved is yours for the taking. Soul-fulfilling relationships, great jobs, passion projects, the works. The universe's guidance is really in motion now, since you're working with its energy and your own natural flow. In this chapter, I will explain what it means to practice your gift and pursue purpose work, suggest ways and outlets to do this, and show the importance of enjoying the growth process so that you're enthusiastic about the life you're co-creating with God.

Lead with Love

I've talked a lot about the vibrational importance of love, but I want to drive home how essential it is to work from your heart chakra when practicing and sharing your gifts. Serving from a love frequency is an absolute priority—not just because it benefits the recipients, but also because your gifts will develop and work faster this way. As a practitioner, you also won't feel as tired and drained when you serve others. Operating from the generous heart chakra will reach more people without even setting that intention. Best of all, when you walk through the world with an open heart, you boost a collective energy that serves every planet in every galaxy.

WHEN TO PRACTICE YOUR GIFT AND START SERVING

Since your morning, night, and impromptu afternoon routines are second nature by now, continue practicing them until Day 15. And after your detox is over, stick with the ritual for as long as you feel called to do it. You're vibrating on a high plane, so you can trust your instincts to tell you if you should continue the full routine, shorten it, skip days, or adjust it any other way to maximize its effects. You want some form of this ritual to keep you in a peaceful, centered, and in-control headspace every day. These practices have changed your identity; they're who you are. Do what it takes to maintain this magical frequency. Life flows easily when you do.

I've positioned these last three days to set you up for a long-term, high vibrational lifestyle that's bursting with love, mystical moments, good health, soul growth, abundance, and inner peace. Though Day 15 marks the end of the program, it initiates a refreshed and recharged existence. When positive emotions motivate and move through you, your body, mind, and soul are energized to serve humanity in a way that's effortless and inspired. And to that incredible end, here's how you can expect your last three days to go down.

On Day 13, please pull out your journal for a fun, freestyle writing exercise to help you narrow down your energetic goals; we'll then plot these on a simpler chart for reference. For now, I'd like you to brainstorm scenarios that elicit the kind of high frequency that you hope to experience on a regular basis—and the type of low energy that you want to avoid at all costs. In my experience, this writing exercise will be largely channeled, even if channeling is not your primary gift. Once you plug into your gifts, celestial answers tend to flow freely from you, regardless of whether you're journaling, advising a friend, talking to a parent, or practicing a gift.

In one paragraph, consider how your life looked and felt before you began this detox program. How did you feel when you woke up? What activities did you do? Who were you most often around? How did they make you feel? What was your environment like? What were your habits? What was your community like? How did you feel before bed every night? Did you ever experience mystical events—and did you know how to interpret them? Did life even make sense? Then, in a second paragraph, please answer the same questions, but write about how you'd like your future to look, now that you've opened your gift with purpose work in mind.

Once you've considered the factors that drag you down and lift you up, I'd like you to create a conscious energetic list—a list of the pain points that plummet your energy and prompts that boost your frequency. To do this, you'll create two columns on a page in your journal. One column will name all the factors that drag you down, and the other will indicate all the stuff that lifts you up. This should come easily, after your writing exercise. Once you make your lists, compare the two sets of priorities. Notice how much you've grown in just 13 days!

To create these lists, it may help to think of specific scenarios and then name the words that apply to how you feel, what you think about, the people involved, the actions you take, and the environment you're in when you're facing that situation. For instance, when you're creating the "Drags You Down" list, you might consider how comparing yourself to others saddens your soul. The rest of the info in the chart becomes easier to imagine and fill out with that example in mind. I've created two simple maps below. Yours will be more extensive than what I've done, but this is a fine starting point to give you an idea of how your lists will look. Got it? Great!

DRAGS YOU DOWN

Emotions
sad , defeated, angry, overwhelmed, rejected, insecure, unlucky

Thoughts
inadequate, unsupported, eager to quit, need to escape

People
spiritual and celeb influencers, dad, boss and colleagues, ex-spouse

Actions
social media scrolling, pull away, call in sick a lot, retreat, people pleaser

Environment
online, mommy play groups, office, ex's house

LIFTS YOU UP

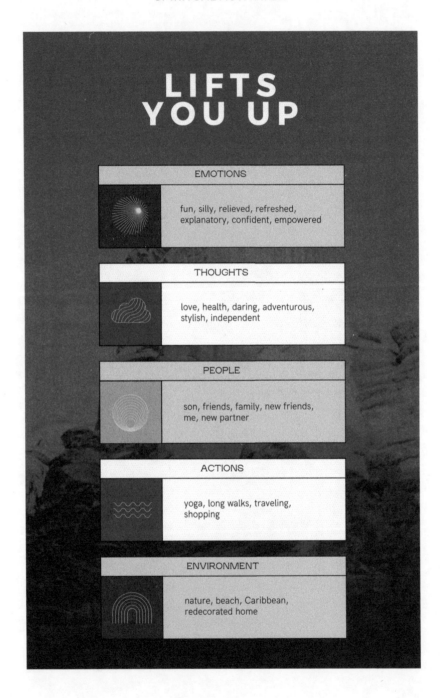

EMOTIONS

fun, silly, relieved, refreshed, explanatory, confident, empowered

THOUGHTS

love, health, daring, adventurous, stylish, independent

PEOPLE

son, friends, family, new friends, me, new partner

ACTIONS

yoga, long walks, traveling, shopping

ENVIRONMENT

nature, beach, Caribbean, redecorated home

What a difference between the two lists! Despite your best efforts to fill your life with all the factors that lift you up, please know that God never intended for life—or you—to be perfect. When your mood or routine occasionally dips into the first list, don't sweat it. Refresh your vibration with a few cleansing and frequency-raising exercises, and keep going. This chart will serve as a prescient reminder of how to live a high vibe life as you serve others.

Moving on to Day 14, this is a two-parter. After your morning routine, state an intention that announces to God that you are ready to practice your gift and explore your purpose work. Close your eyes, take a deep breath, and say something like, "I am ready to step into my gift and purpose work. Show me the clearest and most efficient path to both." It's important to announce your intention with passion, determination, and by really feeling the words as they come out of your mouth. For more emotional emphasis, you can say your intention aloud. You can also record yourself saying it on your phone and play it back for encouragement. A lot of clients write their intentions in a journal, draw a picture around it, and put it in a special box. What matters is that your intention fills your heart, bursts into the world, and makes you feel empowered. Your higher power is in your corner and knows that you're good and ready to do your soul's thing.

The language you use to create your intention statement is important here. Many spiritual teachers insist that you use present ("I am") or past ("I was") tenses to position your brain to process your intention. It's said that if you feel enough emotion while declaring an intention and/ or imagining what the intention will look like, your brain won't know the difference between an event taking place now and what you're creating for the future by emotional thought alone—and this will encourage it to come to fruition. At Authentic Living, we don't endorse this line of thinking. You can't trick your brain, or emotions for that matter, to believe that something is happening when it clearly isn't; your mind is way too smart for that. Beginning an intention by saying you "are ready," or asking God for help, resonates more deeply with the mind since there's no oppositional energy. That's when your mind gets on board.

After stating your intention, I'd like you to meditate on your statement, and to help manifest it into reality, imagine yourself practicing your gift in multiple environments—with as many senses as you can. It's also a good idea to drown out all outside sensory input or meditate to music that moves you and matches the emotions you'd feel while using your gift and doing purpose work. When thinking about your service, it can range in size and outreach, so you may want to begin with a small vision, and as time and your vibration changes, grow it into another goal and another one after that. Expect your gift and work to tweak and evolve, as you do.

After meditating, you will lean heavily on your intuition about what your next steps should be to practice your gift. Working with your gift is like strengthening an energetic muscle—it takes time to build force and consistency. While some might be ready to start practicing right out of the gate, others may require more instruction. Either way, I suggest that you spend at least a week in meditation, increase your self-care (exercising, massages), and pay attention to your dreams—all with the intention of downloading info on how to use your gift. If you feel pulled to begin experimenting, test your skills on friends, family, and pets who won't criticize or judge your progress too much. You can also find a private teacher to mentor you, get your hands on books that move you, visit crystal stores, and talk to as many spiritual folks as you can. At Authenti-cLiving.com, we offer various classes that help you hone your gifts and pursue your purpose work. Ask God for signs that validate or guide you on how to practice your gifts, and then follow the breadcrumbs that appear. Because you've opened your gift and the universe has heard your intention, trust that the right teachers and opportunities will cross your path.

On Day 15, the final day of your detox, take one bold move toward pursuing your purpose. Just like you considered themes in your past that pointed you toward your spiritual gift, I'd like you to do the same when considering purpose work that's right for you. What activities and types of people already bring you fulfillment, gratification, and peace? Do you love helping animals? Do you feel at home working with children or the elderly? Are you happiest when you write or make art? The great thing about purpose work is that while you can use it to become a great healer or renowned channeler who writes books and lectures to thousands, it doesn't demand that you do something "big" in the eyes of others. You can pursue it within your family, your community, or job. Controlling the weather while on a family vacation is a huge plus!

On your final detox day, take your high energy thoughts from this brainstorm and turn them into high frequency actions. Contact a website designer, outline your next steps, make a list of partnerships, buy a new desk—basically, I want you to start doing things that align with your intentions, since this is a new chapter of your life. You may feel drawn to edit your daily to-do list, instead of acting on choices that feel right in your soul. You may also feel inspired to quit your job or serve as a side hustle until you build enough confidence to practice full time. No matter how you get started, your purpose work doesn't need to swallow your entire life. If you really like your job, fold your gift into that, or use your open heart and high vibration to touch the lives of strangers at a nursing home or on the street. It's all up to you. Since you've set an intention at a high frequency, aligned action will solidify your gifts in any context. You don't have to jump in with both feet, but God is calling you to at least splash around in the shallow end.

Get Your Hands Dirty

To perfect my gift, I practiced my skills in different surroundings and with various subjects—colleagues at work, strangers at conferences, family during the holidays, and a few mentors throughout the years. This strengthened my abilities and hinted at environments where I'd eventually feel most comfortable serving (corporate settings, large audiences, intimate gatherings, one-on-one . . .). I suggest the same for you! Also, remember that *your intuition already knows how to do this*. You aren't learning a skill from scratch but catching up on one that your soul learned before you incarnated. Release how you think your gift should act or look. You've received an energetic infusion from God—it doesn't get more perfect than that.

So don't hang a shingle, charge for your gift, or print business cards until you *know* that your gift is polished, you're ready to serve, and you're emotionally prepared to "out" your ability to the world.

Once word travels that you can hands-on heal, channel, tap into the Akashic Records, talk to dead people, or read a stranger's future, your calendar will fill up—fast! Here are a few ideas to feed your high vibe energy and inspire your spiritual journey during this time.

- Travel to a spiritually inspiring place, like Sedona or Costa Rica
- Spend a full day following only your intuition's instructions (this is fun!)
- Visit a spiritual or metaphysical store, and hang out with the owner or other shoppers
- Ask mentors for crystal and book suggestions
- Find online meditations that align with your gift and purpose work
- Create a music playlist that fills and speaks to your heart
- Take classes specifically geared toward perfecting your gift
- Start building a like-minded, spiritual community. This is crucial for support and guidance

PURPOSE WORK IN ACTION

Pursuing a feat as major as pursuing your soul's purpose might feel a little heavy or intimidating at first. I get that. But don't feel put off, because this is work that you were destined to do your whole life. And as we've discussed, it can take any shape and size to suit you. Be creative!

When you use your gift on a local level, you have the ability to touch more lives than you may think. My client Maurine, who has psychic abilities, used them to become an "animal whisperer" in her community. After taking an in-person workshop, she began to telepathically communicate with all kinds of pets to help their owners resolve curious medical and behavioral conditions. She found that folding this gift into her existing job was enormously fulfilling. Another client worked as a small-town dentist and used her gift as a transmuter to calm down her patients' energy when they were in her dental chair. Yet another workshop attendee who was a stay-at-home mom opened up her ability to access the Akashic Records. Her children had unusual behavioral issues at the time, but with this new insight, she was able to recognize that their actions pointed to various spiritual needs and gifts. She now knows how to help their anxiety and hyperactivity, because she has access to detox techniques; she also knows that their affinity for "imaginary friends" is related to psychic abilities because the records said as much. Finally, Mom knew that their wild, outdoor-loving nature is an act of energy clearing and natural wiring, because she learned it during our time together. This allowed the mother to support and help her children grow in new and inventive ways that she'd never considered.

On a larger scale, I really loved privately working with the wife of a very famous motivational speaker. Her goal was to feel more spiritually connected to the universe and optimize her own spectacular gifts. By the time we got to Day 13 of her detox, I helped her activate her gifts as a channel and projector. Though she'd worked mostly behind the scenes with her husband prior to meeting with me, after our training, she began to make appearances alongside him onstage. She now conducts blessings, meditations, and inspirational talks during his sold-out shows. What's more, she feels less drained when working with her own clients and is still energized to help random strangers because she pulls inspiration from the universe.

Over the years, and with the help of Akashic readers, I've come to learn that a person's purpose work can be tied to lessons they feel they're meant to learn on this plane. These lessons either point directly to your purpose or underscore it in some way. For instance, if you think your lesson is to rise above abandonment, you might choose to learn this lesson by using your gift to start a support group that lovingly counsels divorced women. If you suspect your lesson is to overcome insecurity, you could serve in conditions that force you out of your comfort zone.

I've also noticed that the most passionately pursued work comes from the need to heal the kind of pain that's caused by situations that hurt *you*. If you've experienced a medical nightmare and you're a healer, it can feel deeply fulfilling to work with clients that have invisible illnesses and feel dismissed by doctors. Or if you've always struggled in romantic relationships and you read the Akashic Records, you might want to serve those who are longing for a soulmate. By loving others through a pain with which you identify, you are working intimately and miraculously with the heart chakra.

THE POINT OF SERVICE

As you now know, purpose work is all about service. It's meant to fulfill your soul but also heal yourself, others, and the world (and not always in that order). I believe that you're serving any time that you positively affect someone other than you. Purpose work is intended to be a beacon of positivity that affects others in the best way. And when you serve others, you serve your own energy because this causes it to elevate. Serving is a deeply impactful, two-for-one deal that way.

On a more global level, service matters because the universe calls us to feed a collective consciousness and the world's vibration with love energy. Every being, on every planet, is energetically connected. If you inspire, heal, or help a family member, that person will not only feel better, but their boosted energy will impact their next encounter. This ripple effect not only raises frequencies on earth but contributes to a grander vibration that makes the world go round.

When you're not serving in a formal way, you can still serve on a regular basis with kindness, humility, generosity, and love toward humanity in general. A family friend named Sarah shared that she struggled through a rough childhood. Growing up, her single, alcoholic mom spent what little money they had on her addiction, and then abandoned Sarah and her two siblings when Sarah was seven years old. The children went into foster care and bounced from one home to the next. Understandably, Sarah's outlook was bleak and her faith in humanity lost. Yet when Sarah turned nine years old, her perspective turned around—at the mall, of all places.

One afternoon while her foster mom shopped, Sarah stared longingly at a carousel that she desperately wanted to ride but didn't have the money to operate. As if on cue, a passing stranger approached the coin machine, dropped a few quarters in its slot, and walked away—all without saying a word. He didn't make a show of this gesture, yet Sarah says *it changed her life*. Anytime she faces a challenge (and she's had a lot, including chronic illness, a deceased husband, and a robbery at gunpoint), Sarah remembers her merry-go-round angel. His kindness reminds Sarah that there is goodness in the world when she has the faith and patience to see it.

Serving others is a lifelong practice that requires a deep and loving commitment, no matter how you choose to express your gifts and heart. Know that as your frequency rises and your abilities grow, your service will change too. Make the most of discovering the skills and opportunities that appear on each vibrational level. Follow God's signs and synchronicities as you climb the spiritual ladder. You'll be guided to work that matches your energy, at that time.

KEEP IT LIGHT

Knowing that positive emotions elevate your frequency and feed your gift, try to practice your abilities and serve others with as much joy and play as you can. Service can feel heavy when it relates to grief, death, or scary illnesses, so try to find a balance between your work's depth and your soul's need for levity. Also, when you begin using your gift and stretching outside your comfort zone, your responsibilities can feel heavy or scary. This makes it doubly important to keep your frequency high and light, because you can only fill others up when you're full first.

Maintaining a high frequency also invites more messages from God. When you're in a low vibration, you won't notice signs and synchronicities as often; an overwhelmed and distracted mind contracts your awareness of what's happening in and around you. Yet when you're on a higher vibration, consciousness opens like a flower. During those hard, first sessions with others, it's crucial to recharge after so that you feel refreshed and open to divine wisdom.

Gratitude is another emotion that keeps you on a high vibration while practicing gifts and purpose work. Oh, how spiritual teachers love to reinforce gratitude. And while I don't want to underestimate how important it is to be humble and appreciative of your higher power, I don't believe that it's essential to feel grateful *all the time*. Life is hard, man. The challenges we face on this planet can really take us down. But if you can keep other high vibrational emotions on rotation—think growth, creation, and possibility—these driving forces can equally fuel your frequency. When I do express gratitude, I find that it's most powerful when I couple it with love. But gratitude doesn't naturally push me or my gift forward. I think our human body craves cheerfulness, curiosity, and silliness—which are as high vibe as gratitude. Emotion drives energy, so any feeling that's high, light, and infused with love will drive your energy up.

Another huge key to keeping you energetically equipped to practice and serve is continuing to manage old and new blocks. When I first began working with my gifts, I returned to Sedona many times to chip away at old, resistant blocks that were only accessible at certain vibrations. I also cleared and healed new blocks along the way. Keep this in mind as you move forward. You'll never reach a day when you are free of all blocks, since you live in a world that pelts you with nonstop challenges—no matter how high your frequency. On earth, you're here to learn, love, and serve in a way that is authentic and elevates your vibration, plus the frequency of others. Sometimes the lessons aren't fun, but we must learn to deal with the fallout.

All in all, there is no ceiling to how incredible you can feel, how high your vibe can ascend, and how expansive your gift and purpose work can be. But as you soar, know this: growth may feel so good that you become tempted to fall into the ego's trap—and this is *certain* to mute or even kill your gift. I've seen it so many times with famous intuitives whose gifts led them to fame and fortune. That's when their ego kicked in, and God knocked their abilities and reach down a few pegs. When you practice your gift for the purpose of status, money, and attention, those motivating forces will overtake the once-beautiful intention of serving others with humility. Modesty is a mainstay in service because service is selfless. There are days I'm serving with my gifts, and it feels so right. I try to memorize that respectful feeling with my mind and body and repeat it the next time I'm practicing so that my ego never gets in the way.

More Resources and Free Downloads

I've put together a transformative mediation called "Higher Self and Purpose," which is designed to help you access your higher self and experience your highest frequencies in order to start discovering and stepping into your purpose work. Download it here:
www.SpiritualActivator.com/purpose

AFTERWORD

Spread the Blessings

CONGRATULATIONS, FRIENDS! YOU'VE OFFICIALLY finished your 15-day detox! How do you feel? I can tell you from my own experience that this cleanse should have made your body, mind, and energy field feel like new. Your gifts have been activated, and you're on the road to serving others with your purpose work. Consider this a fresh beginning, an energetic do-over. You should feel clear-headed, light in spirit, and motivated to change lives for the highest good of all. You are also keenly aware of how different it feels to walk through the world with pure energy, rather than a mucked-up field. You can sense when you or others are spreading toxins, and you have the tools to eliminate them and sustain a high vibration so that you feel and do your best.

So spread your light and spread the word about how your life has changed! Also know that if you ever feel "off" or your gifts seem rusty, you can repeat the detox. No shame there. Embrace the fact that you've worked incredibly hard during this program, and you deserve every ounce of happiness and abundance that your field now attracts. You have the unlimited potential to find pleasure within yourself and bring joy to others. What a stunning way to live.

As you continue to practice and serve with your whole heart, remember this too: *the light within you is the solution to the darkness around you.* No matter what happens around you, your light will shine when you bring your gifts, service, and love to otherwise daunting situations. You're a limitless force for good and change on this planet. You're beyond letting others negatively affect you because your light will now outshine theirs. That's the power of a detox.

A SPECIAL INVITATION

Join the Spiritual Activator Soul Family

I KNOW WHAT IT is like to feel alone in this world. To feel different or that you don't belong. To have to keep your ideas and your truth to yourself in fear of being judged or rejected by others. The truth is you are not alone. There are people just like you who are on a spiritual journey to find themselves and understand the meaning and purpose of life at the deepest levels. Special souls who are looking for more clarity, peace, freedom, fulfillment, purpose, abundance, and wellness in their lives. People who don't want to settle in life and believe that things can and will be better.

That's why I created the Spiritual Activator's Soul Family. This is a supportive, loving, and growth-oriented community with members from all over the world who have come together to collectively raise the vibration on this planet. This is the place to continue learning more about energy, your spiritual gifts, and your purpose here on this earth. I created this space with the intention of it being a community where its members would serve one another, hold each another accountable, offer perspectives about this book's teachings, love on one another and lift each other up with the power of the knowledge of this book and beyond. I knew it would be an incredible place to be seen, be heard, learn, grow, heal, unlock your untapped potential, and give back.

Just go to spiritualactivator.com/family and request to join and share your intentions with souls that may have already read the book, are in the midst, are revisiting it, or like you, just getting started! I am known for creating some of the most supportive, nonjudgmental, and magical communities on social media, and I, along with my amazing team, will be in there posting, answering questions, and going live often to support you with not only the lessons in this book, but a new way of life. I can't wait to see your first post!

Love,
Oliver

ACKNOWLEDGMENTS

I'D LIKE TO THANK everyone who contributed to this book and to my ability to share its message to the world. Writing this book has been one of life's greatest gifts, and I can only hope that the information here changes your life, in the best of ways.

To Christel Hughes and Nick Stojanovski, for opening my eyes to energy and spirituality.

To Amma (Sri Mata Amritanandamayi Devi), you are the embodiment of pure and unconditional love on this planet.

To Reid Tracy, Patty Gift, Melody Guy, and Lindsay McGinty at Hay House: Thank you for believing in my work. You've all been very supportive and loving every step of the way.

To Kristina Grish, for the countless hours we spent together making this book a reality. You are a natural healer.

To Laura Nolan, for helping take care of all the "details" and making the publishing process so efficient so I can focus on creating this book.

To Mona Loring and the entire Conscious Living PR team, thank you for helping me get my message out there.

To Tony and Sage Robbins, for paving the way for what's possible with purpose work. It's an honor to serve.

To Tim Kring, your heart and desire to impact global consciousness is truly rare. Your work has been a great inspiration earlier on, my friend.

To Gwyneth Paltrow, your authenticity, kindness, and energy is a gift that keeps on giving. Thank you for all your support.

To Julianne Hough, you are a bright and shining light in this world. Watching you step into the dance floor of life, and own it, has been amazing to witness.

To Kim Richards, I'm glad to have met you. You are a bright light in this world. Thank you for all your support.

To Sarah Hudson, the songs you write shift and impact so many. Your vibration is elevating and awakening consciousness at a deep level. It's an honor to know you.

To Donna Karan, your deep love for humanity, and your missions to bring calm in times of chaos, is very admirable. Thank you for all your support.

To James and Kimberly Van Der Beek, for all the fun times with the kiddos and conscious conversations about parenting and holistic living. You, my friends, are all integrity to the deepest levels.

Deep gratitude and appreciation to Laura Dern; Kyle Richards; Demi Moore; Tallulah, Scout, and Rumer Willis; Peggy Rometo; Gerard Butler; Lisa Bonet; Jenna Dewan; Stacy Keibler; Odette Anable; Tobie and Tony Gonzales; Lisa Garr; Blue & Bari—I deeply value you all.

To Mikki and Nadia, your bravery is admirable, and your friendship invaluable. I've learned so much throughout the years.

To Marci Shimoff, you're a gem in this world. A walking embodiment of love, humility, kindness, and purpose.

Acknowledgments

To Nick & Alex Ortner, you both are changing the world with tapping. It's an honor to know such passionate change-makers for humanity.

To Dr. Sue Morter, your passion to help people discover and use the healing power within is amazing to witness.

To Christina Jimenez, your passion for protecting children is something I'll forever be grateful to you for. You're the definition of gladiator in a suit. Thank you for all you do.

To Daniel Raphael, so proud of you brother, keep shining your light and changing lives.

To Peter Nguyen, soul brother in the path, thanks for all your guidance and love. It's fun changing the world, together.

To Tracy Ahearn, your guidance and messages have helped us tremendously.

To Anthony William, for all your loving support and for everything you do for humanity. YOU are the salt of the earth. Your work touches so many lives, and I'm blessed to have you in my speed dial and my life.

To Meleah Rae, for helping us bring our vision to reality with your operational brilliance. Our mission wouldn't be where it is today without your help.

To Nicole Doyle, you bring love to food and all you do. We are lucky to have you as our chef, herbalist, confidante, stylist, and friend. And Jason, my veggie king brother, I'm excited for all that's unfolding this year.

To Fatou, Stephanie, Kat, and all my Geo Love Trainers who help me bring light and love to the souls that need it the most. Watching y'all step into your purpose and brave the unknown with me has been a pleasure.

To Kathy, Wayne, Chuck, Jess, Jenn, Candice, Yvonne, Den, Honey, Juan, Wendy, Elle, Matt, Doug, Sean, and the team that keeps Geo Love Healing spinning. Thank you from the bottom of my heart.

To Chris De Vera, for being by my side through thick and thin.

To Mandy, my love, I wouldn't be here shining my light and stepping into my purpose without your loving nudge and unconditional support. You brought my faith back in humanity.

To Vian, for bringing to this world an embodiment of love frequency.

To Mom, for being a pillar of strength and embodiment of love in our family.

To Dad, for teaching me the importance of perseverance, resilience, and faith.

To Pia, Elaine, Liezl, and Claudine, for being the best sisters any brother could dream of. Each and every one of you hold a unique key to my heart.

To Braydon, my first born. I am blessed to be your dad. To know you is to love you. I am so very proud of you. And to Zion, watching you grow daily is life's greatest joy.

To my Geo Love family, for helping me spread more light in the world, and for trusting me in your spiritual journey.

To God, archangels, higher level guides, and beings of love and light who have guided me in my spiritual journey to date,

I love you all.

ABOUT THE
AUTHOR

OLIVER NIÑO—an entrepreneur, energy healer, and spiritual activation expert—is the creator of Geo Love Healing, an online company designed to help individuals master their energy, unblock themselves, and become healers. Oliver has performed more than 20,000 one-on-one healing sessions, has done group healings with 6,000+ people at the same time, and has trained over 2 million students in 60+ countries in his energy healing methodology. A highly recognized energy healing expert, Oliver and his brand have amassed a loyal, global following including many celebrity clients such as Gwyneth Paltrow, Demi Moore, Gerard Butler, Laura Dern, Nina Dobrev, Jules Hough, James Van Der Beek, and Tony Robbins.

To learn more about Oliver and his work visit:
www.spiritualactivator.com

NOTES

NOTES

NOTES

NOTES

NOTES

NOTES

NOTES

NOTES

We hope you enjoyed this Hay House book. If you'd like to receive our online catalog featuring additional information on Hay House books and products, or if you'd like to find out more about the Hay Foundation, please contact:

Hay House LLC, P.O. Box 5100, Carlsbad, CA 92018-5100
(760) 431-7695 or (800) 654-5126
www.hayhouse.com® • www.hayfoundation.org

———

Published in Australia by:
Hay House Australia Publishing Pty Ltd
18/36 Ralph St., Alexandria NSW 2015
Phone: +61 (02) 9669 4299
www.hayhouse.com.au

Published in the United Kingdom by:
Hay House UK Ltd
The Sixth Floor, Watson House,
54 Baker Street, London W1U 7BU
Phone: +44 (0) 203 927 7290
www.hayhouse.co.uk

Published in India by:
Hay House Publishers (India) Pvt Ltd
Muskaan Complex, Plot No. 3,
B-2, Vasant Kunj, New Delhi 110 070
Phone: +91 11 41761620
www.hayhouse.co.in

———

Let Your Soul Grow

Experience life-changing transformation—one video at a time—with guidance from the world's leading experts.

www.healyourlifeplus.com

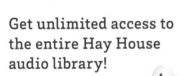